HAWAII
THE ISLANDS OF LIFE

HAWAII
THE ISLANDS OF LIFE

*The Nature Conservancy
of Hawaii*

BY

Gavan Daws

WITH CAPTIONS BY

Dr. Samuel M. Gon III

PUBLISHED BY

*Signature Publishing
Honolulu*

Produced and published by David A. Rick
Signature Publishing—Honolulu

First Edition October 1988
Second Edition November 1988
Third Edition November 1989
Fourth Edition November 1991
Fifth Edition November 1992

Library of Congress Cataloging in Publication Data
Daws, Gavan. Hawaii, the islands of life
Includes bibliography
1. Biotic communities—Hawaii. 2. Ecology—Hawaii.
I. Nature Conservancy of Hawaii. II. Title.
QH198.H3D38 1988
574.5' 09969—dc19
ISBN 0-943823-01-3

Printed in Japan

Table of Contents

DEDICATION 6

INTRODUCTION 7

FOREWORD 9

ACKNOWLEDGEMENTS 11

SPONSORS 13

HAWAII IN THE PACIFIC 14

I   CHAPTER ONE—VOLCANIC ORIGINS 16

II   CHAPTER TWO—COASTS & SEA CLIFFS 36

III CHAPTER THREE—DRYLANDS 64

IV   CHAPTER FOUR—STREAMS & WETLANDS 86

V   CHAPTER FIVE—RAIN FORESTS 104

VI   CHAPTER SIX—SUMMITS 136

REFERENCE MAP 152

PHOTOGRAPHY CREDITS 154

SELECTED READINGS 156

DEDICATION

To the native plants and animals of the Hawaiian Islands,
and to people everywhere who are committed to preserving
the best of our natural world for future generations.

Introduction

Our island state combines spectacular scenic beauty with one of the most varied landscapes on earth. It is a richness that people who live here find almost impossible to leave—a richness more than six million people from all over the world come to the islands each year to discover and enjoy. Where else on our planet can you stand on the slopes of a snow-capped mountain and look below to the clouds that embrace slopes covered in tropical rain forest? Look just slightly further and you can follow orange, hot, molten lava as it slides into the steaming ocean, creating new land.

In the pages of *Hawaii: The Islands of Life* you will see all this and more. The Nature Conservancy of Hawaii has put together one of the most fascinating books ever written about Hawaii. For the first time, the full extent of the remarkable natural diversity of these islands is showcased. From sun-drenched coastal dunes, we move up volcanic slopes, glimpsing a variety of living things—Hawaiian plants and animals that make Hawaii a truly unique part of the United States and the world.

I join with The Nature Conservancy in hoping that as all of us learn how intertwined our future is with the thousands of native species whose islands we share, we will work harder to protect them.

I have long been a proponent of the dictum, "Think global, act local." Living on islands at the crossroads of the Pacific, we have always kept one eye on Asia and one on the western world. That global perspective is essential to our success, and perhaps even to our survival. Yet in many ways, global impact depends on the action we each take at the local level. It is right here in Hawaii that each of us must act, and act quickly, if we hope to pass the richness of our natural heritage on to future generations.

I am pleased that in the State of Hawaii we have begun planning and management work on our Natural Area Reserves. Consisting of 18 of Hawaii's finest natural areas and encompassing more than 100,000 acres, the Reserves are part of the natural legacy we treasure: the native flora and fauna that shaped early Hawaiian culture and are today a living link to that ancient and proud tradition. These natural lands also protect our forested watersheds, the lifeblood of our economy, and are an irreplaceable part of the scenic beauty which captivates residents and visitors alike.

The story of *Hawaii: The Islands of Life* reminds us that our islands, and our planet are too small and too fragile to take for granted. I hope that this book will motivate each of us to help protect what has taken millions of years to evolve. What we do in our generation, together, will make all the difference.

John Waihee
Governor
State of Hawaii

THE GENEROUS COAST OF MOLOKA'I is a beckoning symbol of Hawai'i and a heritage worthy of protection.

Foreword

AFTER HIS SECOND HEART ATTACK, at the age of forty-four, my father bought some land and retired to the island of Moloka'i, twenty-six miles across the channel from the growing city of Honolulu on the island of O'ahu. From that time on, although my brother and I had to attend school in Honolulu, we spent as much time as we could on Moloka'i, immersed in the sheer, immediate beauty of that quiet island.

We always knew we were extraordinarily lucky. We loved exploring Moloka'i's rain-forested mountains, waterfall-laced sea cliffs, isolated valleys, and miles of open beaches.

And fishing! Fishing with my father and mother was an experience. They each held world records that stood for more than twenty years: Mother for the 'ahi (yellowfin tuna) she caught off the coast of Wai'anae, and Father for a 16.8 pound 'ō'io (bonefish) he caught at Kaupoa Bay on the west end of Moloka'i. It's wonderful fishing in those waters.

The Hawaiians say there's something magical and healing about Moloka'i, and I believe it. My father never had another heart attack, and he lived in good health to the age of seventy-four.

THE WORLD MOVES A WHOLE LOT FASTER now than it did when World War II was winding down and we were growing up. Of course, some things stay the same: you still can't find a single stoplight on all of Moloka'i, even in "downtown" Kaunakakai.

But we sensed it then, and we can see it more clearly now: things are changing, even on Moloka'i. For the native plants and animals on Moloka'i, and on all the Hawaiian Islands, the isolated habitat that has supported and nourished them is changing thousands of times faster than nature prepared them for. Scientists predict that within the next ten to twenty years at least half of the native Hawaiian plant and animal communities we know today may be lost forever, unless we do something soon to protect them.

The Nature Conservancy of Hawai'i is doing something. Working with scientists and other concerned people throughout the state, the Conservancy identifies Hawaii's rarest and most threatened natural areas. Once these areas have been acquired—by gift, exchange, purchase, conservation easement, or management agreement—the Conservancy maintains them as public trusts, providing conservation management and encouraging their scientific, educational, and recreational use.

Since 1980, The Nature Conservancy of Hawai'i has been responsible for the protection of thousands of acres of Hawaii's most important natural lands, ranging from the windswept coastal dunes of Mo'omomi on Moloka'i to the lush, tropical rain forests of Waikamoi on the slopes of Maui's magnificent volcano, Haleakalā.

These preserves not only protect thousands of species found nowhere else on earth, they also provide for essential human needs. The rain forests of Kamakou Preserve, for example, supply sixty percent of Moloka'i's water; and Waikamoi Preserve protects watershed serving most of upcountry Maui. Hawaii's scenic beauty and rich cultural heritage are also safeguarded in these magnificent protected lands.

And there are other compelling human reasons for protecting "islands of life" in today's great sea of change. Scientists are finding that each wild species is like an encyclopedia of genetic information capable of providing humankind with new solutions to life's challenges. According to the *Medical Tribune*, "There are perhaps thousands of chemical compounds in common plants and fungi that could become effective new weapons in the war against disease." Some we know already include digitalis, quinine, morphine,

10

and penicillin. Are we prepared to throw away whole libraries of knowledge we haven't even begun to investigate? Without protection for our natural lands and wildlife, we may never know the value of what we are losing.

The Nature Conservancy of Hawai'i, with the help of thousands of members and supporters, will continue working to save diverse lands and wildlife found only in the Hawaiian Islands. But there is so much more to be done.

You have already joined in our efforts by buying this book, the proceeds from which will all go to protecting land in Hawai'i. I hope you will want to continue to help protect the amazing diversity of life we have been so fortunate to inherit, so that we can pass it on to future generations.

The world is changing too fast for us to rely solely on what poet Carl Sandburg called "the saving minority." To keep pace, each of us must do our part. Together we can keep alive the plants and animals that share our world; and as my father once proved, nature in turn can help keep alive what is best in our own lives.

Samuel A. Cooke
Chairman
The Nature Conservancy of Hawai'i

PLACES WORTH PRESERVING exist on each of the Hawaiian Islands. Wellsprings of cultural, biological and scenic richness, places such as Waikolu and Kamakou on Molokai enrich our lives in a myriad of ways.

Acknowledgements

IMAGINE WALKING THROUGH A HAWAIIAN RAIN FOREST. A canopy of bright red ʻōhiʻa blossoms is above you, and at your feet, roots meander across a trail packed with wet mosses and small ferns shining in dappled sunlight falling between the trees. The air smells different here. Cool fragrances of growing plants and rich earth combine and drift through the forest with the moist freshness of a mountain breeze. A crimson ʻapapane darts by, searching for the perfect ʻōhiʻa blossom, leaving a song for you.

Those of us who have been fortunate enough to enjoy Hawaii's wilderness have searched for ways to share the experience with others. The Nature Conservancy of Hawaiʻi opens a number of its preserves to the public, and there are many other opportunities to hike in Hawaii's federal and state parks and on mountain trails. But you can't always get to a pristine rain forest—at least not as often as you'd like to, and possibly not at all.

Hawaii: The Islands of Life is our way of sharing the rain forests and other natural wonders of Hawaiʻi with you. We hope the book will help many more people enjoy Hawaii's special, wild places. We also hope that getting to know these natural areas and the wildlife that survives there will create in each reader a desire to help protect them.

The protection of Hawaii's natural resources depends upon many organizations and individuals, and our acknowledgements would be incomplete without an expression of thanks to these colleagues. In particular, Senator Daniel K. Inouye, Representative Daniel K. Akaka and Governor John Waihee have provided the leadership for a new era of government protection of our unique natural hertiage.

Because it is the result of a group effort, *Hawaii: The Islands of Life* is symbolic of the way The Nature Conservancy works here in Hawaiʻi and across the country. Scientists and artists, environmentalists and corporate executives all have been important partners in this project.

Funding for the book came from three of Hawaii's most generous and committed corporations. We are grateful to Alexander & Baldwin, Bank of Hawaii, and Duty Free Shoppers Group, Limited, for their strong support and concern for the future of Hawaiʻi. Thanks to their contributions, proceeds from the sale of the book all go to protect land in Hawaiʻi. In addition, their support enables The Nature Conservancy to offer a year's free membership with every book sold.

Thanks are also due to the biologists whose intelligence and dedication made this project a reality. Sam Gon's depth of knowledge of Hawaiʻi and of biology are reflected in his sensitive photo captions and in portions of the text. Alan Holt's love of the land and breadth of knowledge have been a prime force behind this book, as well as many of the accomplishments of The Nature Conservancy in Hawaiʻi.

Other specialists whose knowledge and willingness to share it have been indispensable include Audrey Newman, for her Laysan Island experience and other help; John Ford, for his intimate knowledge of streams; Joel Lau, for his sensitive descriptions of Hawaiian habitat; Russ Apple and Reggie Okamura for sharing material on the life of Thomas A. Jaggar; George Balazs and Stewart Fefer for checking facts; and Bill Mull and Frank Howarth for photographs and facts on life in lava tube caves.

Many others contributed time and energy to the project: Doc Stryker, advisor and mentor to The Nature Conservancy since its inception in Hawaiʻi, kept the project on track from beginning to end. Trustee Catherine Shen volunteered her time as a project editor and consultant, and Carol Fox orchestrated the writing and production. Norah Forster assisted author Gavan Daws in Canberra.

12

Experts on Hawaii's natural history, Cam and Kay Kepler reviewed manuscripts and sent materials all the way from Georgia. Charlie Lamoureux provided important insights in several areas, and Beatrice Krauss, Hannah Springer, Steve Montgomery and Wayne Gagne also contributed their special expertise. Wayne's sudden loss reminds us of the transience of all life. His dedication to Hawai'i and to conservation served as an inspiration to us all.

Above all, the project would not have been possible without the help of the dozens of photographers who believe in what The Conservancy is doing and were willing to spend hours combing their collections for their best shots. Their names are listed later in the book. David and Bonnie Muench deserve special thanks for dropping everything and coming to Hawai'i to provide exceptional photographs where existing material had proven insufficient. The work of Richard A.

Cooke III and his wife, Bronwyn, has been important to this book and has helped to advance the cause of conservation in Hawai'i in many ways.

Overseeing the entire production was trustee and long-time supporter Gaylord H. Wilcox, who worked closely with publisher David A. Rick to turn our ideas into reality.

Partnerships with the sponsoring corporations and with all the organizations and individuals mentioned above, with the Trustees of The Nature Conservancy, and with thousands of individuals who have contributed to The Nature Conservancy helped make *Hawaii: The Islands of Life* possible. They are joined in spirit by everyone who has ever loved these islands. It is partnerships such as these that will make it possible for us to pass this precious natural heritage on to future generations.

Kelvin Taketa
Executive Director
The Nature Conservancy of Hawai'i

PARTNERSHIPS in conservation make it possible for us to pass our precious natural heritage on to future generations. . . .

THE SUN RISES OVER MOLOKA'I, *unveiling Hawaii's islands of life.*

*"In our hands now lies not only our own future,
but that of all other living creatures with whom
we share the Earth."*

David Attenborough, *Life on Earth*

HAWAII IN THE PACIFIC

THE HAWAIIAN ISLANDS EXIST in the most profound oceanic isolation on the face of the globe—more than two thousand miles from the closest continental land mass.

Beginning seventy million years ago, the islands emerged as volcanoes from the sea. On average, only once in every one hundred thousand years was a new life-form able to find its way to the islands and establish itself.

Time and distance allowed the emergence of an amazing array of plants and animals, thriving in tropical rain forests, on lowlying drylands, among sunstruck coastal dunes, and deep in lightless lava tubes. Most of these life forms are seen nowhere else on earth. The Hawaiian Islands would have astonished Charles Darwin.

Hawaii: The Islands of Life is the story of an intricate set of life forms evolving in splendid isolation, and what happens when these life forms are confronted with momentous challenges from powerful outside forces.

THE NATURE CONSERVANCY of Hawai'i is active in protecting lands throughout the Hawaiian Islands. As seen here in a photo taken from the Space Shuttle and beginning with the foreground bottom left are the islands of Ni'ihau, Kaua'i, O'ahu, Moloka'i, Lāna'i, Kaho'olawe, Maui and Hawai'i: biological gems in the middle of the great Pacific Ocean.

CHAPTER ONE
Volcanic Origins

THE ONLY WAY TO GET TO KNOW A VOLCANO, Thomas Jaggar believed, is to live with it.

He built his home on stilts, wedged into a crack in an immensity of dark volcanic rock on the southeast flank of the island of Hawai'i—latitude 19° 5′ 47″ N, longitude 155° 15′ 37″ W—at an altitude of four thousand feet, precisely so that he could go to bed at night and wake in the morning snug within the rim of the most continuously active volcano in the world.

After breakfast he would stride through the mountain mists to the cliff face of the crater of Kīlauea and clamber two hundred feet down a rope ladder, to stand with nothing between him and the firepit Halema'uma'u. Here he was, Thomas Augustus Jaggar, Jr., a human being of the early twentieth century, with his blood heat set by evolution at 98.6 degrees Fahrenheit, wearing the necktie of a serious volcano scientist, measuring the level of a perpetual lava lake that simmered and bubbled and fumed in his eyes. Molten lava, pushing right up at him out of the earth's magma, eighteen hundred degrees and more at the surface. Primordial heat, searing the bare skin of his unbearded, unguarded face.

Jaggar loved to teeter on the very edge of personal physical scorching. He lived and breathed volcanoes. He sniffed his breakfast egg with its faint sulfurous smell and wondered if the egg of all life might be volcanic in origin, if evolution went back beyond the living embryo to the chemistry of volcanoes— sulfur, hydrogen, oxygen, carbon dioxide, ingredients of the egg, ingredients of the volcano.

HOT, FLUID, AND EFFERVESCENT, lava from Pu'u 'Ō'ō hurtles a thousand feet upward—a vent for gases held under terrific pressures in vast chambers beneath the island. The eruptive vent typifies Hawaiian volcanoes: spectacular fountaining and fast-moving flows sending lava miles downslope to the sea, adding to the growth of the geologically infant island of Hawai'i.

He smelled out volcanoes wherever they were on earth. At Bogoslof in the Aleutians he saw hot lava tumbling into the ocean, the beaches aroar with sea lions, the steaming air above screaming with birds, life and deadly volcanism flourishing together. At St. Pierre in Martinique, molasses and Caribbean rum flowed like lava in the streets after Mount Pelée laid waste the town in 1902, and Jaggar saw human beings dead by the hundred, close up, a baby dead in an iron cradle, a big fellow dead on his back in a deep baker's oven—the flesh shriveled and drawn away from his joints by the heat—not of baking but of volcanism. In Japan he had himself rowed out in a little skiff to look down over a hot lava tongue licking the sea floor below. He trailed a thermometer in the boiling water. All about him floated dead fish, belly up, boiled. If the tiny boat should capsize, Jaggar—the pre-eminent American volcano scientist of his day, with three degrees from Harvard and a worldwide reputation, geology professor to the young Franklin Delano Roosevelt—would boil. He loved every moment of it.

In the furious world of volcanic eruptions Kīlauea was as gentle and generous as a volcano could be, active almost perpetually, giving out especially liquid lavas that often fountained spectacularly, making for wonderful viewing, but not normally going off with a deadly bang. People most times ran toward Kīlauea to watch, rather than away for their lives. And when the volcano was quiet tourists could saunter down into Halema'uma'u with an egg in a pan and fry it on moving lava, and write home about this strange, entertaining breakfast, being sure before mailing their postal card to scorch its edges a toasty Halema'uma'u brown.

Everything that made Kīlauea an ideal tourist attraction made it ideal for continuous scientific study—Jaggar's life passion. Early in the twentieth century, when he was climbing to the world peaks of his profession, only one permanent volcano observatory existed on the face of the earth, at Vesuvius. Jaggar argued that the United States should have its own observatory, and for the sake of the best science it should be located at Kīlauea. There, as nowhere else in the world, a volcano could be studied in all its phases—before, during, and after eruptions. And the resident observer—of course—should be no one but Thomas Jaggar. Jaggar was the primordial force behind the Hawaiian Volcano Observatory. He started work in 1912, in a little seismometer vault dug out of ash and pumice, rimside, five minutes from his house. He observed nonstop. He was forever designing new monitoring instruments (though none of them ever matched the fine tuning of his collie dog, Teddy, a domesticated sensing device who always knew before anyone else when Kīlauea was preparing to perform). In good times Jaggar could readily raise research money, public and private. In bad times he raised pigs to meet the payroll. Good times and bad, he published scientific papers continuously, like an intellectual lava flow from Kīlauea, an outwelling that pushed the world science of volcanology ever forward into the twentieth century.

Jaggar had a wife named Isabel. On his endless expeditions across newly cooled volcanic rock she looked after the food. She took dictation for his close-up eye-witness reports of eruptions. Thomas died before Isabel. She had his body cremated, respectably committed to controlled flame, and later, when she felt the moment was right for her own private ceremony, she secretly scattered his ashes in a greater fire—the perpetual fire of Jaggar's life, Halemaʻumaʻu at Kīlauea.

ALWAYS THINK IN MILLIONS OF YEARS, said Jaggar, and everything is in motion to one who senses slow motion. Think of the Hawaiian archipelago in million-year motion.

The islands, all of them volcanic, were formed in turn by upwellings from an eruptive hot spot below the ocean floor.

Then in turn they were rafted away with the slow, slow movement of the huge Pacific Plate over the earth's mantle, seventy million years of geological time travel, north and west across the Tropic of Cancer, worn by wind and rain, sinking gradually under their own weight as they went, oldest first, back beneath the surface of the sea.

Today there are eight major islands and more than one hundred twenty smaller islands, pinnacles, reefs, and shoals. The oldest and farthest to the north and west have disappeared below the sea and are now underwater seamounts. Kure and Midway are atolls with coral reefs and highest points of no more than a few score feet. More than fifteen hundred miles south and east of Kure, offshore of the island of Hawaiʻi, a new island is forming. Still a half mile and several thousand years of time yet below the ocean surface, it already has a name: Lōʻihi.

Most recently emerged of the main islands is Hawaiʻi, often called the Big Island. Shaped by five volcanoes, it shows the huge creative force of volcanism. Mauna Loa, still active, rises more than twenty-nine thousand feet from the ocean floor, thirteen thousand, six hundred seventy-seven feet from sea level to summit. It is ten thousand cubic miles in bulk, meaning it is the biggest single volcanic structure on earth—a hundred times bigger than Shasta or Fujiyama, indeed the biggest such feature in the solar system anywhere between the sun and the planet Mars.

THE HAWAIIAN CHAIN EXISTS in the most profound oceanic isolation on the face of the globe, more than two thousand miles from the closest continental land mass.

Life had to come from far away, blowing in on the winds, floating in on ocean currents, rafting in on logs swept from the continents, touching down with migratory birds on their trans-oceanic flights.

MOLTEN ROCK CONGEALS into a frozen yet fluid form as a small tongue of pāhoehoe lava feeds from the edge of an active flow.

In this sterile island world of volcanic rock and salt spray, plants established themselves only at the rate of perhaps one species in each hundred thousand years. No amphibian or land reptile successfully crossed the ocean to Hawai'i. No oak, no pine, no sequoia. No big game animal came from America or Asia, nor any beast of burden. In seventy million years only two mammals settled in: one for land, a hoary bat, solitary, nocturnal, reddish-gray and weighing less than an ounce; and one for sea, a monk seal of primitive habits.

The volcanic shapes of the islands were sculpted by wind and weather, and a varied physical foundation was laid down upon which an enormous range of life forms developed. A mountain peak on Kaua'i, Wai'ale'ale, is the wettest spot on earth (at least the wettest where anyone has maintained a rain gauge). Other, higher summits—Haleakalā on Maui, Mauna Kea and Mauna Loa on the Big Island—are alpine stone deserts. Within a few miles of each other on any of the main islands there may be tropical rain forests, lowlying drylands, sunstruck coastal dunes, and lightless lava tubes.

In these extravagantly varied habitats immigrant species adapted, and new species evolved, life forms never before seen on earth. One kind of drosophilid fly became eight hundred. Three hundred fifty kinds of immigrant insects evolved into over ten thousand native Hawaiian species. Twenty species of land snails became a thousand. Two hundred fifty flowering plants became eighteen hundred. The silversword colonized from bog to cinder desert. The 'ōhi'a lehua found ways to live almost everywhere, from new lava to ancient bog, and in the process took on an abundance of different forms. And the native Hawaiian honeycreepers changed so much as they adapted to the wide range of island habitats that they would have astonished Charles Darwin.

In the biological history of Hawai'i these are the big, sweeping developments, landmarks of worldwide significance. Other native creatures developed more modestly, but no less remarkably. Crickets by the shore, so adapted to salt spray that away from it they cannot survive. In the rain forest, carnivorous green caterpillars. At the extreme freezing height of a stone desert summit, the *wēkiu* bug, so finely adapted to cold that if you take it in your hand—blood heat 98.6 degrees Fahrenheit—its proteins cook.

All of this development and change occurred over millions of years. Plants and animals between them created soil, soil trapped moisture, moisture allowed more and more growth, until forests appeared which influenced climate. In all the different ecological zones of Hawai'i, particular groups of interrelated species clustered together. These groups developed into something that was more than the sum of their parts. They were interrelated, interactive, interdependent, promoting each other's survival. They became, in other words, natural communities.

And these elegant associations became numerous. In less than sixty-five hundred square miles of land mass, there can be identified more than one hundred fifty kinds of natural communities, each community a small island of life harbored within the larger islands of life that are the Hawaiian Islands.

Following page: NIGHT AND THE VOLCANO, a primordial scene of island-building, with land born out of darkness in rivers of fire and plumes of smoke.

ALONG A RIFT ZONE A FIRE CURTAIN RISES. Where it falls, life is burned away. Despite the lava behind and the sulfurous fumes before it, a patch of vegetation near Puʻu ʻŌʻō persists—a kīpuka—an island of life surrounded by barren lava.

PĀHOEHOE LAVA, flowing in ropy swirls, sweeps through a lowland forest. The lava cools around the trees even as they burn, forming tree casts and converting a living forest into stone sculpture.

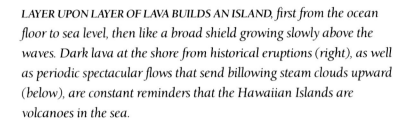

LAYER UPON LAYER OF LAVA BUILDS AN ISLAND, first from the ocean floor to sea level, then like a broad shield growing slowly above the waves. Dark lava at the shore from historical eruptions (right), as well as periodic spectacular flows that send billowing steam clouds upward (below), are constant reminders that the Hawaiian Islands are volcanoes in the sea.

ROARING, HISSING, AND CRACKLING, molten lava encounters the sea at Kalapana. In a flash, water becomes superheated steam and glowing lava becomes stone.

CREATION AND DESTRUCTION
are linked as a lava flow from
Puʻu ʻŌʻō moves through a patch
of ʻōhiʻa forest. The unburned
section becomes a kipuka—an
ecological island in the midst of
volcanic devastation.

ON COOLED PĀHOEHOE LAVA so fresh it bears a golden, glassy skin, a crevice traps wind-blown debris and moisture from fog—and the first new plant life appears, a young ʻōhiʻa lehua with an ʻōkupukupu fern.

A PRIMITIVE LIVING LANDSCAPE, tree ferns (background) dominate a misty lava plateau. Their fronds provide shaded protection for smaller plants, such as young ʻōhiʻa lehua (center), and a variety of ferns and lichens (foreground). Old fronds fall, adding to the soil accumulating in crevices. Once life is established, it grows on itself.

AN INFANT FOREST BEGINS ITS LONG LIFE, as spindly ʻōhiʻa trees of identical age stretch upward over a lava flow newly clothed with vegetation. As the ʻōhiʻa trees mature, they continually change the character of the landscape, taking it from low ferns and lichens toward a forest climax.

THE SUCCULENT FRUIT of the ʻōhelo are often the only expression of moistness on the harsh lava terrain. The low shrubs that colonize lava flows begin the slow transformation of barren landscape into a community of life.

IN LESS THAN A HUNDRED YEARS, when conditions are right, a lush forest of ʻōhiʻa lehua trees and hāpuʻu ferns stands where lava devastation once prevailed. The volcanic setting in Hawaiʻi creates a dynamic cycle of destruction and renewal, creating changing opportunities for life.

32

A CRICKET of the lava tube spends its life in perpetual darkness. Delicate, eyeless, wingless, pigmentless, it scours the floor of the huge lava cavern for organic debris. Like other Hawaiian lava tube animals, it has adapted to a subterranean habitat so geologically recent that we must rethink our ideas on how fast species can adapt.

A LAVA TUBE FORMS as pāhoehoe lava moves through a rain forest. Trees above the tube are still erect, holding their leaves, but they are doomed, their roots seared away by the furnace below.

ROOTS OF 'ŌHI 'A LEHUA TREES grow down into a lava tube, seeking moisture, forming a delicate curtain on which an entire biological system in the cave depends. Eyeless planthoppers feed on the scarlet roots, and are in turn eaten by blind spiders. On the cave floor, root debris is consumed by pale crickets. No two Hawaiian cave ecosystems are exactly alike; each is an island of life. Any disturbance overhead, from a new lava flow to feral goats grazing above, can end life below by disrupting the energy supply flowing down through the root curtain.

A CRICKET OF THE OPEN LAVA FLOWS was recently discovered on the island of Hawai'i. Specialized for life on fresh lava, it feeds on organic debris constantly carried by steady trade winds onto the otherwise barren flows. Nearly wingless and altogether flightless, it nevertheless finds its way onto fresh lava flows soon after they cool.

Following page: FROM THE COAST TO THE HIGHEST SUMMITS, Hawaiian landscapes are volcanic landscapes, originating in fire and desolation, then clothed and ornamented with life.

CHAPTER TWO
Coasts & Sea Cliffs

ONE OF THE LARGEST SEABIRD COLONIES in the tropical world, for diversity and sheer numbers, is in the Hawaiian Islands.

During quiet times there you might not quite register this, you might be aware of nothing more than the music of waves on coral sand and the sound of the albatrosses clashing their beaks as they dance, and you might well doze off.

Your eyes would be opened by the sooty terns. Suddenly one day they appear, by the scores of thousands, darkening the sky. Then they are on the ground, laying their eggs. After that, every day at dawn, they all go up in the air at once, making a tremendous racket. No need for a morning alarm, just lie there and the sooty terns will go off. And at dusk off they go again.

The Hawaiian monk seal ignores this. It lolls all day on the beach—looking for shade, settling into moist sand, flippering to the water to cool off, shifting up the dunes at night to sleep out of reach of the waves. That is its routine, for months at a time.

The female Hawaiian green sea turtle has her own precise interest in sand temperature. She comes ashore in the dark of night, silently, to lay her eggs, setting them in the sand at a depth where heat and moisture are exactly right for hatching. By morning when the tern alarm goes off she has departed, leaving only her flipper tracks above the tide mark.

All this on a single Hawaiian island. But not within hundreds of miles of urbanized Honolulu. The green sea turtle egg does not tolerate human presence; just the heedless thump of five-toed feet on sand above can abort a hatching below. The monk seal wants to breed in privacy away from humans. And the sooty tern, the albatross, and the fourteen

A WINDOW ON THE PAST, the dunes of Moʻomomi show the Hawaiian coast in a largely unaltered state. Wave-eroded sea caves reveal layers of ancient sand turned to stone, preserving fossil bones.

other breeding species of that immense seabird colony—all congregate on a tiny raised coral atoll, Laysan, highest point perhaps forty feet, latitude 25° 42′ 41″ N, longitude 171° 44′ 06″ W, part of the state of Hawaiʻi, but uninhabited and more than eight hundred sea miles northwest of Honolulu.

THE FIRST MEN ON LAYSAN in the nineteenth and early twentieth centuries were sealers, guano diggers, feather collectors—all takers. And then, with the idea of contributing, a man from Honolulu introduced rabbits. What he contributed was devastation. Within twenty years the rabbits ate virtually everything green on Laysan all the way down to the nubs, turning the atoll into a sand desert, just four of the twenty-five plant species surviving in small numbers and several bird species pushed to extinction by having their habitat gnawed out from under them.

A scientific expedition came in 1923 to get rid of the rabbits. One day the shooters spotted three birds, Laysan honeycreepers. The next day a sand storm blew up, gale force, and stung and buffeted all three birds to death—the last of their kind on earth, the only songbirds in the documented history of the world to go extinct within sight and sound of humankind, with the time of the end recorded to the hour.

Over the next few years the Laysan teal also came to the very brink of extinction. In all the world these birds lived only on Laysan, around a small lagoon, no more than a couple of square miles of habitat. They stepped among beach morning glory and sedge, puddled about potholes feeding on insects, and were never sufficiently shrewd about evading humans. The guano diggers slaughtered them, because they were there. By the 1920s, after those introduced rabbits had done their worst to Laysan's green growing things, there were many more teal skinned and stuffed in the world's museums than

BLOOMING in the early light, the morning glory pōhuehue winds through a bed of ʻakiʻaki grass.

live ones left around their home lagoon. In 1930 a man from Honolulu found a last individual, a female, fluttering about, perhaps decoying him away from her nest. He found the nest with its clutch of white eggs—and every last shell was punctured by the beak of a raiding curlew.

Yet the teal of Laysan survived. How? Well, by biological providence the female had enough semen in her oviduct to fertilize a second clutch of eggs. At least that is the story, and of course it is a wonderful tale of biological brinkmanship.

Did this small reproductive miracle actually occur? Or did the man from Honolulu simply fail to spot the male of the pair? Or was there another female hiding silent and motionless on her nest in the bunch grass? The true answer has blown away on the Laysan wind.

At any rate, after the last rabbits were killed the island began greening again, bird habitat came back, and within another twenty years—happy ending—the teal was on its way to recovery.

These days Laysan is legally protected from unthinking intrusion by twentieth-century human beings. It is once more a tiny window opening upon the biodiversity of the past. The window is small and distant, but through it can be glimpsed an island of life.

ON ALL THE EIGHT MAIN HAWAIIAN ISLANDS, where a million twentieth-century human beings live, there is no place like Laysan. Yet one spot that does offer a sense of what Hawaiian strand and coast were like before the time of our species is a stretch of sand dunes called Moʻomomi on the island of Molokaʻi.

Moʻomomi remains remote, uninhabited, a wild place. Walking there among great onshore riffles of wind-swept sand, you can easily find spots where the dunes have lithified—turned to sandy stone. And here erosion by wind and wave may bring to the present-day surface evidence of endemic native life forms long dead: shells of land snails, fossil bones of birds, an eagle, a giant flightless goose, a thick-billed crow, a long-legged, bird-eating owl.

Moʻomomi gives off a strong sense of uninterrupted connection with the old, the ancient, the slow motion of evolutionary time moving within the yet slower motion of geological time. No human beings live there. And that is precisely why, every so often, coming out of the northwest islands, there will appear at Moʻomomi a monk seal, looking to do nothing; or a female Hawaiian green sea turtle, to dig a perfectly conceived hole in the sand and lay her eggs by night; or a Laysan albatross, to cruise on the salty winds that blow forever over the dunes.

AMONG THE COASTS OF THE MAIN ISLANDS, Moʻomomi represents extremity—the last strand, so to speak. Another kind of Hawaiian coastal extremity is found on northerly shores; soaring sea cliffs of fluted wet basalt, those of Molokaʻi rising as high as three thousand feet—the highest in the world.

And alive on a stark cliff face you may spot a single human being, at the end of a hundred feet of knotted one-half-inch nylon rope, hanging in the wind with a two-thousand-foot fall to the rocks below. This is Steve Perlman, doing extreme work, pollinating the rare, disappearing, endemic Hawaiian plant *Brighamia* with a paint brush.

In the old days forests grew right to the cliff edge, and perhaps the natural pollinator of *Brighamia*—a honeycreeper, a large moth, no one really knows—would come out of the forest and flutter down the wind to find its flower of choice. Now in many places the forests do not reach the cliffs, and anyway the pollinators are rare in the forests. So, late in the twentieth century, Steve Perlman has taken it upon himself to do their work.

From a kayak offshore he scans the cliffs through binoculars. He sights *Brighamia*, never more than a small population, perhaps only a single individual: he is willing to work one on one. He comes in on the surf to tackle the cliff climb, with altimeter, cutting knife, Japanese split-toed shoes that fit well to the rocks, recording notebook and pencil, seed-collecting bag, a single sandwich, two bottles of water for the thirstiness of the day's labor, a flashlight against having to stay late at work, and two lengths of rope, one to reach the *Brighamia* he has sighted, the other in case he sees something else exciting when he gets there—all that way out on the cliff face he would feel foolish coming up twenty feet short.

With his brush he collects pollen from the throat of the *Brighamia*, paints the stigma, and goes roping from plant to plant, cross-pollinating. Months later he returns, the same laborious roping way, to collect the seeds that have filled their capsules to bursting. Back in civilization he puts the seeds into cultivation, preserving *Brighamia* against a possible time in the future when wild habitat might be restored for them and their natural pollinator. A long-term holding operation. For other rare and endangered Hawaiian plants he does the same, wherever he finds them, up high in a drenched Hawaiian bog or hundreds of feet down some dryland gulch. In the islands of life this individual man has found his particular niche. The brush he uses is a regular painter's tool of trade, and he is an artist, a solo virtuoso of extreme habitat, one of a kind, *Homo sapiens, Explorator perlmanii maximus hawaiiensis*, willing to go to the extreme edge to bring native Hawaiian plants back from the brink. ❧

A CHALLENGING environment is met by Hawaiian coastal plants facing arid, salt-laden winds that carve away the landscape. The plants take on forms that fit their setting, unmistakably shaped by the sea.

HAD DARWIN SEEN THE LAYSAN FINCH, he would have known that his observations in the Galapagos Islands applied to Hawai'i as well. The birds have adapted to differences in food sources, the size of their bills matching the size of the seeds where they live.

DESCENDANTS OF THE "LAST LAYSAN TEAL," a pair of the birds feeds on a cloud of salt-loving Hawaiian shoreflies that breed in huge numbers in Laysan lagoon. The lagoon's sun-baked waters are saltier than the surrounding ocean—one of the few hypersaline lakes in Hawai'i.

FULL OF HISTORY AND A DIVERSITY OF COASTAL LIFE, Laysan atoll is a small remnant of land, a coral flat sitting on a submerged volcano. Yet there are species of birds on Laysan that are found nowhere else, inhabitants of this isolated island of life.

VYING FOR THE ATTENTION OF MATES, *male 'iwa birds inflate their red throat pouches in a nesting colony shared by red-footed boobies (left). These colonies, once widespread, now remain only on remote offshore islands and atolls.*

COURTSHIP AMONG THE ALBATROSSES OF LAYSAN. Shaking their heads about with bills thrust upward, this "skycalling" is seen only in the albatross colonies of the northwest Hawaiian chain and in very few refuges around the main islands.

Following Page: THE INCESSANT CHURNING OF THE SEA wears away at the windward coasts, leaving sea cliffs and rocky remnants of the ancient shoreline, such as Puʻu Pehe, off the coast of Lānaʻi.

WEIRD SHAPES *echo a forested past at Moʻomomi. Fossil root casts attest to vegetation where none now exists, a hint of the extent of Hawaiian lowland forest in ancient times.*

AN ANCIENT *raiment (right) of native vines adorns the shoulders of a coastal bluff on Oʻahu. Fragrant white flowers of the hinahina and delicate lavender pāʻū o Hiʻiaka sit amidst orange ʻilima blossoms. This rich mixture of native plants is a rare sight nowadays, but tattered, still-beautiful remnants can be enjoyed on a few remote beaches.*

MOUNDS OF SAND ON AN IMMACULATE BEACH *mark the burrows of sand crabs (ʻōhiki) dug at night. In the darkness, the crabs scour the sand for seaweed and other organic debris washed in on the waves.*

PAST ONLY THE FIRST TRIAL OF LIFE, *a sea turtle hatchling scurries from its sandy nest, past the snapping beaks of hungry seabirds overhead, to hide in the cool foam of incoming waves. Now it must face the ocean's challenges. Someday it may return to the same beach to dig a nest in the warm sand.*

WITH MATURITY *comes time for relaxation in the remote, protected waters of a refuge lagoon. Adult Hawaiian green sea turtles return to the same beaches where they hatched years before, now large enough to resist most of the ocean's dangers.*

LOLLING NEAR A SHADY RETREAT, a Hawaiian monk seal regards its surroundings. Two red-footed boobies roost above him, under the cloudless skies of the Northwestern Hawaiian Islands. Now protected, the monk seal was pulled back from the brink of extinction and still teeters near the edge: an endangered species.

BROODING ITS SINGLE EGG *in one of the few trees growing in the French Frigate Shoals, a black noddy, or noio, also nests on rocky ledges and cliffs on the main islands.*

50

IN A REFUGE FROM PREDATORS *sooty terns, or ʻewaʻewa, nest in a colony on Midway Island. As ground-nesters, they cannot persist where cats, mongooses, or rats hold sway. Where free from those threats, they punctuate flat, sandy areas with evenly spaced nesting territories, emitting an incessant chorus of calls.*

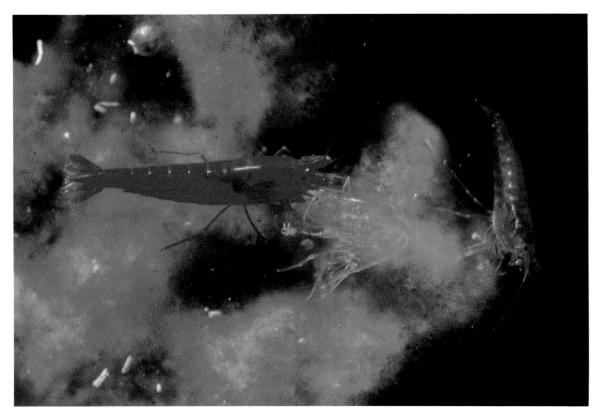

A FRAGILE DENIZEN OF TWO WORLDS, the 'ōpae'ula are shrimps found in unusual brackish pools scattered along the lava coasts of Hawai'i and Maui. These anchialine pools are the surface windows on a strange ecosystem: a water-filled network of cracks and crannies connected to the ocean deep underground. In these lightless, nearly oxygen-free waters, the tiny 'ōpae'ula spend much of their lives. They emerge into algae-rich anchialine pools to feed, sometimes in such large numbers that the water seems to turn red.

*SEPARATED FROM THE SEA ABOVE GROUND, but connected below, the anchialine pool called Luahinewai
receives a mixture of fresh groundwater and salty ocean waters. Ancient trails lead to this pool, which was a
source of drinking water. Fluctuating with the tides, the pool reveals its underground connections with the
sea. It is habitat for many unique Hawaiian species, some of which are extremely rare.*

WATERFALLS PLUMMET FROM SEA CLIFFS hundreds of feet high on the Hāmākua coast of the island of Hawai'i. Vegetation clings tenaciously to steep hanging valleys and along the bases of cliffs, battered by landslides and storm waves. Such sea cliffs are called pali lele koa'e: "cliffs where the tropic birds soar."

GROWING 2,000 FEET ABOVE THE WAVES, Brighamia, a rare Hawaiian coastal lobeliad, has white tubular flowers (above). They are a tantalizing view, perched on the sea cliffs of Molokaʻi, the highest in the world. The ālula has relatives on another set of sea cliffs on the island of Kauaʻi; hundreds of miles distant.

FRAMED BY LICHEN-COVERED LAVA, *a rare mā'oli'oli sends up a round cluster of flowers. Above it, a flowering 'ilima grows on a thinly soiled ledge. Coastal cliffs provide some of the rarest Hawaiian plants with their last refuge, out of reach of introduced goats, and seldom seen except at the end of a long rope.*

ON PARENTAL GUARD a pair of masked boobies flank their ungainly offspring, still thickly clad in fuzzy white down. Nesting on a barren patch of ground, the birds persist only on offshore islets and other predator-free locations.

57

58

THE NORTH COAST of Molokaʻi
receives the full brunt of the
ocean, carving the tallest sea
cliffs in the world. Large valleys
such as Pelekunu open onto the
sea, feeding nutrients from the
land into the ocean.

ATOP A STEEP-WALLED STRONGHOLD *a rare forest of native loulu palms holds sway.* *Known from only this sea stack, called Huelo Rock, and from two small patches on the* *nearby sea cliffs, the loulu forest is almost never visited nowadays. In earlier times,* *Hawaiians climbed the cliffs of Huelo for sport, and used the large fan-shaped fronds of* *the loulu palms to slow their leaping descent to the ocean; an early form of hang-gliding* *not practiced today.*

Right: FLUTED, *razor-backed ridges of Nā Pali catch the morning sunlight on the north coast of Kauaʻi. Skirts of coral sand washed against the base of the cliffs build up during the summer, but are swept away by winter storm waves.*

A CRATER LAKE FILLS AGAIN after a decade of drought, and a rare Hawaiian fern, 'ihi'ihilauākea, sends fronds up from the lakebed to cover the surface with emerald green. Known from only two locations in the world, both on the island of O'ahu, it was once more widespread in the islands. The ferns, superficially resembling four-leafed clover, undergo a wild burst of growth and reproduction after rare storms drench the dry leeward coast.

SALT SPRAY MISTS THE CLIFFS OF MOKIO near Mo'omomi on Moloka'i. The coastline appears timeless in the late afternoon light, making it hard to imagine that the coasts and lowlands have seen more change than any other Hawaiian natural area.

CHAPTER THREE
Drylands

IN THE HOT HAWAIIAN SUMMER OF 1854 the Frenchman Jules Remy went on an excursion to the northern and western parts of the island of Moloka'i, canoeing along the coast past the valley of Pelekunu to the peninsula of Kalaupapa, climbing the cliff trail to Ho'olehua, taking a horse to Mo'omomi, to the beach at Kepuhi, then making his way back over the low West Moloka'i summit of Pu'u Nānā and down again to the south coast at Kaunakakai.

Remy did not enjoy himself much. He had to share his canoe with a seasick man, and ashore the man continued landsick. At Mo'omomi the wind blew stinging sand in Remy's eyes, and he did not venture in among the wild dunes. At Kepuhi there was only brackish water to drink and either this or something he ate upset his stomach, so that on the ride back across the island to Kaunakakai, through arid dusty uninviting territory, he felt poisoned all the way. He did not give the Moloka'i drylands high marks for picturesqueness.

Scientific value, though, was something else again. Remy was a naturalist, and on Moloka'i, poisoned stomach or no, he botanized nonstop, gathering Hawaiian plant specimens, rejoicing when he found something rare, and noting every name in botanist's Latin: *Lobelia, Scaevola, Lysimachia, Euphorbia, Vaccinium, Phyllanthus, Cassytha, Sesbania, Dodonaea, Myoporum, Gnaphalium, Chenopodium, Lepidium* . . . .

Traveling on horseback across Hawaiian terrain in midnineteenth century, Remy was well into the era of introduced livestock in the islands. He was able to fill his specimen bags and his notebooks and his naturalist's mind to overflowing. But in fact the dry landscape through which he rode was emptying out of native plant species almost literally beneath his horse's feet.

Remy's ride took him only a few days, no time at all in the annals of science. But by the chances of history he became the first Western scientist to do any systematic botanizing in the Moloka'i drylands. And simultaneously he was the last to see with a scientist's eye any significant stand of dryland forest on West Moloka'i.

Even at that, much of the forest was already gone before he got there. To reconstruct in his mind anything like a whole dryland natural community on Moloka'i, Remy had to think back to forested land that he had seen earlier in his Hawaiian travels, at Kaupō Gap on East Maui.

Later observers had to do even more extensive mental reconstruction, because on all the main islands ever more of the drylands were being transformed from their original condition. As late as 1860, the people of Kula on Maui got their water for drinking and farming from fog drip. But the forests of leeward Haleakalā were being cleared, and Kula became a much drier place. Offshore of Maui, the small island of Kaho'olawe once produced its own cloud cover. But its forests were cleared and came to be seriously over-grazed by cattle and goats, wind and rain tore at exposed soil, and the whole island went virtually treeless, parched and barren.

These days, more than a century and a quarter after Remy's ride, the range of the drylands has been irreversibly diminished. For one thing, scores of thousands of acres have been cleared and planted in sugar cane and pineapple. Recovering an overall idea of the drylands is like the demanding task of reconstructing some vanished culture from the sparse evidence of pottery shards or slivers of fossil bone.

Still, a sharp observing eye can do a lot. Start on the

A LONE GUARDIAN ON THE LAVA FIELDS, a wiliwili tree provides only temporary shade as it flushes with leaves shortly after the sparse winter rains. During the driest parts of the year it stands as leafless as the dead, sun-bleached branches of the 'a'ali'i that once grew near it. Crusty lichens on unweathered boulders are the mark of the Hawaiian dryland ecosystem.

leeward side of an island, always drier than the windward side, and at low altitudes very dry indeed. Look inland to the mountains and it may be raining high up, but not much of the rain gets this far down the leeward slopes. Summer is the driest time of all. Native annuals go brown and die, trees and shrubs jettison their leaves to save water, and plants that do keep their leaves stop growing to wait out the dry spell.

Then come back after the first rains of winter, when the drylands do get watered, and the color is green. Shrubs and trees quickly leaf out. Many plants are blooming. In Hawai'i native birds are often brighter than native blossoms, but up close all kinds of flowers can be seen.

Lift up your eyes to higher ground, often with more rock than soil showing, sparsely vegetated, and there on weathered lava flows or bouldery talus slopes you may see remaining pockets of native Hawaiian dry forest, especially where twists and turns in the terrain produce a northern exposure.

Higher again you can see mesic forest, moister, with a much greater variety of tree species and a denser, more tangled understory. Here you may pick out the distinctive stands of one of the classic native Hawaiian trees, the *koa*, with its grey-green rounded crown and its limbs sometimes covered with lichens subsisting off fog-borne moisture. And often enough, in among the trees, there will be a population of native Hawaiian birds, red and green honeycreepers and the fly-catching *'elepaio*.

Every piece filled in on the jigsaw puzzle of your mind shows more and more of the drylands' past as one of former riches of native plant and animal species. No single species of tree was dominant in most dryland forests; there were diverse combinations. More species of native birds used to exist in dry forest than are found today in upland rain forests. For Hawaiian biodiversity, acre for acre, these dry forests and shrublands offered the most.

WITH A SINGLE red blossom, a native hibiscus, koki'o 'ula'ula announces itself on the dry cliffs of Mokulē'ia, O'ahu, its simple beauty heightened by the austere setting.

Finally, if you are willing to go the extra distance, walk the extra mile, you can still see stretches of dryland much as they once were; for example, in the upper reaches of the Wai'anae Mountains on O'ahu, or on Lāna'i, at Kānepu'u, where an early ranch manager put up fences against roaming cattle, salvaging a unique forest of native persimmon, *lama*, and olive, *olopua*, spiced with the rare Hawaiian gardenia, *nā'ū*. And on steep, rugged slopes at Pu'u o Kalī above Kīhei in Central Maui, the deciduous *wiliwili* tree still flourishes in quantity, its swollen trunk decorated with bright orange native lichen, its branches bursting forth in season with light yellow or salmon blossoms.

In such places you can get some sense of what dry forests meant in the biological history of the islands. They were the hardy communities of trees and plants that extended organic life to sterile leeward slopes. They made their gains slowly and with effort, over long, long periods of time. Their gains made possible more gains—soil built up, moisture retained, more seeds germinating, more trees growing, more moisture attracted—more transformation of Hawaiian volcanic rock into islands of life.

ONE OF THE GREAT RECOGNIZED RESOURCES of the drylands in the early nineteenth century was sandalwood. By the time of Jules Remy's ride the big stands were just about all gone, cropped out in only a few decades, to be sold on the Chinese market at Canton—at least the most highly fragrant species, the most commercially desirable. But sandalwood is rugged, a survivor, and several species held on, even on the island of O'ahu where the trade was most hectic. Today you can walk trails not all that far from Honolulu and find sandalwood growing sturdily.

Still tucked away in remote parts of the drylands are other potential resources for the twentieth and twenty-first centuries. *Ma'o* shrubland is found on dry red weathered clay, in places where it rains as little as ten to twenty inches a year. *Ma'o* is a shrub that grows two to six feet high, bringing forth bright yellow blossoms after the seasonal rains. It is a form of cotton, in the same genus as American commercial cotton. *Ma'o* by itself would not make a commercial crop. Its fibers are too short. But just because it evolved in a singular way, remote from the mainland, it has a striking usefulness to the commercial cotton industry, only recently realized.

The leaves of mainland long-fiber cotton exude a sweet nectar that attracts insects, and there are ants that "farm" these insects for the honeydew they produce. For cotton growers these infestations mean insect-ravaged plants, more use of pesticides, and higher costs. The Hawaiian *ma'o* developed in mid-Pacific isolation without ants and these associated insects, and its leaves produce no nectar. Put the attributes of the commercially desirable, long-fibered mainland cotton together with those of *ma'o*, which does not attract ants and other insects, and the combination amounts to a net gain for the industry. A hybrid has been developed and is available to mainland growers looking to cut down the use of pesticides and the costs that go with it.

Ma'o is found nowhere else in the world but Hawai'i. You can see it in any number of places, though mostly only as a scattering of plants among congregations of weeds. But here and there, beyond the point where dusty roads give out, or by the shores of remote bays like Keōmuku on Lāna'i, *ma'o* grows in abundance, in association with native plants such as *pili* grass, *'ilima*, and the *nehe*, a Hawaiian relative of the daisy.

Unnoticed or disregarded, *ma'o* would go the way of any number of other dryland plants, to endangerment, to extinction. Attended to and studied in all its Hawaiian particularity, *ma'o* carries a message, and the message is that maintaining diversity of species is by no means merely an exercise in the biology of nostalgia, but part of the ongoing life of the islands in their fruitful connections with the rest of the world. 🐦

WHEN THE WILIWILI bloom, the blossoms are the only adornment on bare branches. With shades from creamy white to crimson red, the flowers mark the coming of the winter rains to the arid leeward flanks of O'ahu.

A HAWAIIAN HAWK PERCHES IN THE CALM of a cloudless day. Now known only from the island of Hawai'i, the piercing cry of the 'io can still be heard in the skies above Ka'ū and Kona.

GLORIOUS YELLOW ON BRANCHES festooned with lichen, māmane flowers delight the eye at ʻUlupalakua on Maui. The māmane tree grows in drylands from near sea level to high cinderlands, supporting many native insects and a rare bird, the palila.

THE BROAD EXPANSE OF HAWAIIAN DRYLANDS is evident on the leeward slopes of Moloka'i. Seemingly barren from afar, each gulch conceals a rich hoard of striking and unusual dryland plants.

*A WILIWILI AND ITS ASSOCIATES FLOURISH immediately after the
winter rains wash the Hawaiian drylands. For a brief time the
drylands are green. Near the base of the tree a native vine, the kūpala,
erupts into growth from seeds lying dormant until the winter rains.*

72

THE SLOW GROWTH of centuries shows in the gnarled limbs of an 'ohe'ohe tree. Like many Hawaiian dryland trees its foliage is temporary, fully expressed only for a month or two after the brief winter rains. For much of the year its grey limbs stand leafless, blending with the sun-baked, lichen-covered slopes.

A FOREST QUIETLY REGENERATES under ancient boughs, as seedlings of a rare Hawaiian gardenia (nā'ū) push through a thick bed of olopua leaves at Kānepu'u, Lāna'i.

WITH JUST ENOUGH WATER TO SUPPORT THEM, a rich assemblage of lichens spreads over a lava boulder. Paradoxically, if conditions were much wetter the lichens could not survive—they need an occasional dry spell to persist.

A RARE 'AKOKO NESTLES IN A LAVA SPIRE untouched by rain, while storm clouds sweep around the West Maui Mountains. Hawaiian drylands and wetlands are often abrupt neighbors, creating habitat contrasts seen in very few other places on the planet.

AS IF ARRANGED by a master, the natural contours of an ancient dryland 'ōhi'a lehua tree frame a scarlet triplet of blossoms. From coast to summit and from desert to bog, the 'ōhi'a seems to flaunt its amazing adaptive range, the most widespread plant of the Hawaiian Islands.

RED-WINGED FRUIT of the ʻaʻaliʻi depend on the wind to spread; they are effective vehicles, for ʻaʻaliʻi shrublands can be found in the dry lowlands on almost all of the main islands.

AN OWL THAT FLIES BY DAY, the pueo is frequently seen soaring above pili grasslands, or roosting quietly on the slopes of Waimea.

COOL EVENING comes to the drylands at Puʻu o Kali. Sunset light accents a wiliwili tree standing over a mix of native shrubs and grasses. The spiny lava has saved this patch of Hawaiian dryland: more-arable lands nearby have been converted to pasture and agriculture.

DELICATE YELLOW BEAUTY of the maʻo (above) unfolds in the cool, pre-dawn air near Hulopoʻe on Lānaʻi. A relative of hibiscus, this Hawaiian cotton blooms along the drier coasts and lowlands (right). Valuable hybrids between Hawaiian and commercial cotton have been produced recently, underscoring the value of natural diversity.

SUNSET LIGHT BATHES A TRIAD OF RARE DRYLAND TREES near 'Ulupalakua: hea'e (left), 'aiea (middle), and halapepe (right). Behind them a small, dense grove of other native trees stands over the southern coast of Maui. The emerald grass around their trunks seems beautiful, but in reality it is their bane. It is kikuyu grass, an introduction from Africa that robs moisture from the native trees and prevents their seeds from germinating.

THE RAREST and the most fragrant of the Hawaiian sandalwoods, the 'iliahi of Haleakalā, today grows only on the dry lava slopes of East Maui. When it blooms, the scent of its deep red flowers mimics that of its fragrant heartwood.

A LOFTY RELATIVE OF THE SILVERSWORD, the iliau bears the same rosette of leaves, but on a tall stalk. Growing only on the island of Kaua'i it graces the canyonlands of Waimea.

THE FLOWERS of the iliau demonstrate their close relationship to alpine silverswords. Both plants flower once then die, sending hundreds of seeds on the wind.

SEEMINGLY OUT OF PLACE, A FERN IN THE DRYLANDS grows from a crack in the lava. Several species of Hawaiian ferns seem to grow only in the drier lava flows, an unusual habitat for plants that normally grow only in the wettest of environments.

A WIND-BLOWN DUNE OF DARK VOLCANIC SAND winds through a dryland forest far from the coast. The sands have never seen the ocean, formed instead during volcanic fountaining. Red blooms of 'ōhi'a lehua hang above the sculpted slope.

A RARE HAWAIIAN TREE THISTLE sports bright orange brushes in a mesic forest on the slopes of the Wai'anae Mountains of O'ahu.

AN UNCOMMON *blend of native trees characterizes the Hawaiian*
dryland forest. Clothed with lichens instead of mosses and sporting
a bewildering array of leaf shapes, there are more kinds of trees in
Hawaiian dry forest than in Hawaiian rain forest.

CHAPTER FOUR
Streams & Wetlands

IF YOU EVER MANAGED TO CLAMBER to the very top of a mountain called Kaunuohua behind Pelekunu Valley on the north coast of Moloka'i—and few human beings have done this—you would have scrambled up four thousand five hundred feet of the steepest imaginable slopes, and you would need a drink of water, badly.

If you knew where to look you would find a little natural hollow scooped out of the solid rock, no bigger than the hollow of a pair of hands, and in the hollow you would find cool, clear water. You would not be able to lower your face close enough to drink. The hollow is too small for that. But you could take the hollow stem of an *uluhe* fern and use it for a drinking straw. You could drink all you wanted, and so could your companions, and so could any who came after you, and you would never exhaust the water. The little secret flow is endlessly replenished from within the rock. The water of life.

Refreshed, you could stand and look down into Pelekunu, and there are very few sights in the world to match the vision of this great, green dreaming valley below you, with its silver stream coursing to a blue ocean.

The main islands of Hawai'i between them used to have three hundred sixty-five perennial streams, meaning that every day for a year you could have gone rockhopping along a different watercourse, each with the characteristic Hawaiian stream profile of riffles, rapids, falls, and plunge pools, always with the hypnotic sound of cascading water in your ears, up to the headwaters where ferns and mosses and lichens adorn the rock faces and everything is soaking wet, including you.

MORE THAN FIFTY MILLION GALLONS of water a day pour from a grand, lush valley into the sea, creating the ideal habitat for native Hawaiian stream animals. One of the last undiverted Hawaiian streams, Pelekunu is protected by The Nature Conservancy of Hawai'i.

On the principle of leaving the best till last, Pelekunu stream and its tributaries in Pelekunu Valley might well qualify for the three hundred sixty-fifth day.

PELEKUNU STREAM IS SHORT, like all Hawaiian streams (the longest is the Wailuku River, at Hilo on the island of Hawai'i, only eighteen miles). And nearly all Hawaiian streams are prone to flash floods. You might be taking your ease in a delightful pool, doing nothing much, like a monk seal of humanity, in bright sunshine with no sign of rain anywhere that you can see, and you might or might not become gradually aware of leaves or flowers or the fruit of the mountain apple floating by you, something that was not happening before. Next thing, the water goes turbid and rises a foot, two feet, three, though the musical sound of the stream has seemingly not changed. Then suddenly out of nowhere comes a shocking flood, with a rush and a roar, huge, a colossal natural bulldozer mass-moving earth by water power, fierce enough to pick up not just little rocks but giant boulders and hurl them down, raking them over the stream bottom and flinging them against the stream walls, with a crashing roar that can be heard for miles, rolling thunder.

Pelekunu subjects you to all this at ultimate levels of intensity. If you work back into the high parts the stream channels become very narrow, the going gets hazardous, the valley walls rise a thousand feet above you, and there is evidence of landslides. Even in quiet times there is an almost constant dribble of small rocks randomly falling. In a big storm big rocks will shear off the valley walls, and as they hurtle down they will take with them huge amounts of soil and vegetation into the watercourse, forming a vast slurry that jets downstream, slamming against the banks as it goes, ripping away more and more and more vegetation, until

88

everything is dumped—thousands upon thousands of tons—at the river mouth.

In Pelekunu the valley and its streams are always making and remaking themselves, just as the active volcanoes of the Big Island do. At the crater of Kīlauea preparatory rumblings may beckon you to come closer to watch a majestic geological event. But in Pelekunu the rolling thunder of boulders breaking loose in a cyclonic storm should be attended to immediately as the most serious of announcements to get out, right now. Otherwise you yourself may become a part of the geological event, and be carried away by it, literally.

NOTHING CAN STOP PELEKUNU IN FLOOD. And even in normal times it always makes its way to the ocean. Elsewhere in the islands other streams come to the sea freely and directly in waterfalls over cliff faces. Others again reach the ocean only as intermittent trickles interrupted altogether in dry times. And there are stretches of coast where no streams at all reach the sea. In some regions of the island of Hawai'i the new volcanic rock is so porous, so permeable, that water is absorbed in great quantity almost instantaneously, and streams hardly get started. This can be seen on the southeastern and southwestern coasts, where not a stream mouth or estuary punctuates the coastline.

Stream life in the Hawaiian Islands has adapted itself to a wide variety of natural circumstances—from the shock of flash flood, to seasonal and annual variations in stream flow caused by drought, to the rigors of the dispersal of larvae between island streams. But major diversions of water to suit urban, agricultural, and industrial purposes can depopulate streams by disrupting the flow of water to the sea. Many species need both the stream and the sea to complete their life cycle.

A big storm in Pelekunu does fierce things to the valley's main stream and its tributaries. Landslides may cause all aquatic life to be wiped out, at least for the time being. But the storm passes, and as the stream begins to carve a new channel through the debris, life comes back: all kinds of freshwater snails, the Hawaiian shrimp, 'ōpae, in plenty, native damselflies, craneflies and midges in amazing abundance, and high up, as far up as thirteen hundred feet, three species of Hawaiian goby fishes, 'o'opu, schooling, as they are seen to do nowhere else in the islands.

The 'o'opu, the 'ōpae, and the hīhīwai snail spawn in the stream, the eggs hatch, and the larvae float down, all the way to the sea. Ocean currents sweep them away along the coasts, into the community of marine plankton. They reappear at

PLUNGE POOLS and waterfalls punctuate the course of Hawaiian streams: formidable obstacles for native fish and shrimp that must migrate up from the sea.

A GROUND NEST was safe for the Hawaiian stilt, or ae'o, until mongooses, rats, and other predators were introduced to Hawai'i. Now all native ground-nesting birds are in jeopardy.

stream mouths as tiny post-larvae, and then in the early phase of their mature existence they fight their way upstream; up that steep difficult Hawaiian stream profile of pools and cascades, inch by inch, the fishes thrusting with their tails and clinging with suction-cup pelvic fins. Alongside them shrimps and snails are tenaciously laddering up the waterfalls on ferns and mosses, up into the permanent fresh water where they will live all their adult lives.

ALL THIS LIFE DEPENDS ON THE FLOW of the streams, and the natural flow of the streams depends on the intricate balance between the falling of rain and the storage of rainfall. Up around the headwaters heavy vegetation cushions the fall of raindrops and allows water to seep into the ground, to be stored behind natural dikes of impermeable rock or to accumulate in perched aquifers above layers of dense lava. Up here springs and seeps can be the start of streams. Lower down toward sea level, immensities of underground fresh water ride on immensities of salt water, and can be tapped by artesian wells. At the coast, fresh water discharges through stream estuaries or else comes out as groundwater, forming undersea springs that well up as coldspots in the warmth of the salt shallows. And in a few places fresh water meets salt in anchialine pools, openings in coastal lava that are neither sea nor stream, a halfway world that harbors a unique fauna of adapted ocean species.

Parts of the Hawaiian Islands get heavier rain than many places in the world. But at the same time the demands placed on stream water and ground water are heavy too, and late in the twentieth century this pressure is being felt by every species that depends upon water—and that means every species inhabiting the islands, from the goby and the 'ōpae and the damselfly to *Homo sapiens*. Perhaps more than any other single element, ready availability of water is becoming the limiting factor in the sustenance and the extension of life, all across the islands, in the streams and out of them.

Of all places in the islands, only Pelekunu has been recognized and given legal status as a nature preserve to protect an entire native stream system and its watershed. It is, so to speak, a motherlode stream for Hawai'i, and indeed for the whole Pacific region. What can be learned and experienced at Pelekunu has a value that can be traced along every stream in the Hawaiian Islands, and in other islands of life elsewhere in the great ocean. 🐚

THE MODEST beginning of a Hawaiian stream trickles through a spring perched high on a lava cliff. Mosses and ferns thrive in the pure and continual flow of water.

NEAR THE SEA, WAIMANU STREAM MEANDERS through its floodplain, a rich estuary containing native sedges and a variety of Hawaiian stream animals. An estuarine sanctuary recognized by federal and state governments, Waimanu, like Pelekunu, is one of the few Hawaiian streams that still runs uninterrupted to the sea.

A LONG ASSOCIATION WITH HUMAN BEINGS allows the Hawaiian stilt, or ae'o, to persist at Pearl Harbor—near a major highway and within sight and sound of O'ahu's main airport. Unfortunately, not all of the islands' native birds are as adaptable.

A DELICATE HUNTER rests for a moment on a streamside boulder. There are more than twenty species of Hawaiian damselflies, each graceful and richly colored. Most of these have aquatic larvae, but a few grow in the moistness held between the youngest leaves of rain forest plants.

THE 'AUKU'U IS A SHARP-EYED STALKER, perched motionless along a Hawaiian stream. It waits for the slightest movement, then spears a small fish or freshwater shrimp with its narrow beak.

SHAPERS OF THE LAND, many tributaries seem to work in concert to create the splendid valleys of the Kohala Mountains on Hawai'i. Slowly but unceasingly, they cut through the thousands of lava flows that built the islands.

WHEN THE RIDGETOPS are lost in clouds, every waterfall finds a voice, and the power of water becomes apparent.

TREADING CAREFULLY ON FLOATING LEAVES, a pair of endangered Hawaiian gallinules, ʻalaeʻula, searches for tender shoots of water plants. Shy and secretive, they are the least common of the native waterbirds.

AN OASIS FOR ENDANGERED WATERBIRDS, Kapoʻikai pond on the island of Hawaiʻi is surrounded by arid lava flats. It is the largest of a complex of anchialine pools at Makalawena, habitat for rare native animals.

AN AMPHITHEATER FOR A CHORUS OF WATERFALLS, the drainage for Waiʻaleʻale, the wettest spot on earth, makes a rare appearance on an uncommonly clear day. Water has deeply carved the island of Kauaʻi, making it an island of gorges and rivers.

*LAKES ARE RARE IN HAWAI'I because volcanic soils are very permeable.
Lake Wai'ānapanapa sits in the crater of a cinder cone, high in
the wettest montane forests of East Maui. It's waters are darkened
by tannins leached from the rich vegetation growing around it.
Eventually, the sedges that ring its shores may fill it completely,
turning it into a bog.*

TWIN RIVERS SCULPT the north coast of Moloka'i. Wailau (left) and Pelekunu streams (right) have worked their way deep into the center of the island, leaving a mountain between them. This mountain, Oloku'i, is one of the most pristine sites in the state, while Wailau and Pelekunu are regarded by many as premiere examples of the Hawaiian stream ecosystem.

LIVING UP TO ITS NAME ONLY PART OF THE YEAR, the 'o'opu hi'ukole (red-tailed goby) sports its mating colors on the stream-bed at Kīpahulu. The rarest of the Hawaiian stream gobies, its presence is one of the best indicators of a healthy Hawaiian stream.

A STREAM SNAIL still tied to its oceanic origins, the hīhīwai is found only in the most undisturbed Hawaiian streams. Its larvae are washed down to the sea where they develop, eventually to crawl the long way back up the streambed to spawn.

HIDDEN BENEATH THE RUSHING TORRENTS of Pelekunu stream is a rich community of aquatic Hawaiian animals originating in the sea and still linked to it in a cycle of water and life.

CHAPTER FIVE
Rain Forests

WHERE THE TRADE WINDS BLOW in off the northern Pacific and encounter the mountains of Hawai'i, at elevations of two to five thousand feet, the air is forever moist. This is rain forest country.

From a distance the forest shows itself to the eye in colors that are unmistakeable, a subtle blend of blue-brown-grey-green. In times of fog or mist or falling rain the light filters diffusely through overarching trees. In times of no cloud cover the sun comes sifting down to the forest floor in a shifting, dappled dazzle of wet silver-gold and green. Out of a carpet of the thickest, plushest moss, tree ferns grow to far above head height for a human, their trunks ten or even twenty feet tall, their fronds unfurling still higher. *'Ōhi'a lehua* trees may rise to a hundred feet, and out of their branches sprout more ferns, herbs, and even other trees and shrubs. Natural diversity begets more natural diversity, things grow out of things that grow out of things, canopies above canopies, understories beneath understories. And when the dominant trees of the rain forest, the *'ōhi'a lehua*, burst out in blossom, the *'apapane*, a Hawaiian honeycreeper with crimson plumage, flies mile upon mile to feast upon the nectar, and the forest canopy is filled to bursting with vibrating life.

At such times—indeed at any time—the Hawaiian rain forest gives off a wilderness sense that everything is in precisely the right place and the right condition of existence, everything connected with everything else, exactly as it should be.

ABOUT ALL THIS THE FERAL PIG CARES NOTHING. In the Hawaiian rain forest these days, the pig is just about everywhere. It has not yet set its cloven hoof upon the extreme heights of Oloku'i on Moloka'i, and it has not hoisted its powerful body up onto the remote plateaus of 'Eke on Maui or Nāmolokama on Kaua'i. But in almost every other rain forest area the pig is present, especially on the windward side of mountains on the main islands, all the way from Kaua'i to the Big Island, in fearsome numbers, perhaps as many as fifty thousand, meaning that for every twenty human beings in modern-day Hawai'i there is a feral pig.

In the rain forest this introduced animal rips up native mosses and chews on native tree ferns for the starch inside of the stems. It devours the three species of native Hawaiian orchids. It churns the earth to get at the roots of other native plants that it favors, and it snouts up earthworms and grubs and eats them. The feeding is excellent, and the breeding is wonderful: if this month you see a given number of feral pigs, in four months time you might see double the number. In short, in the pig's scheme of things, Hawaiian rain forest is nothing but a fabulously rich system for converting intact wilderness into rampant pig.

The pig likes introduced plants just as much as it likes native plants, and this is where things start to get desperately serious for the rain forest. Strawberry guava, which has been in the islands for decades, doing increasingly well for itself in a variety of habitats, has lodged in the rain forest. The pig enjoys it. A passionfruit vine from South America is a more recent introduction. Brought to Hawai'i as an ornamental, it has turned out to be superbly equipped to climb *'ōhi'a lehua* trees, engulfing and suffocating them, and in the process wiping out understory. The pig has a big appetite for passionfruit. The pig eats and moves on, and guava seed and passionfruit seed move with it, journeying with the pig through the rain forest, traveling through pig gut and pig bowel, to be dispersed and fertilized in one movement.

BURGEONING WITH LIFE AT ALL LEVELS, from the forest canopy awhir with birds to the smallest fern on the moss-covered ground, the Hawaiian rain forest is a vibrant, primeval pattern. As water is its lifeblood, so the rain forest is vital watershed for Hawai'i.

Hawaiian rain forests are full of island species that have had life to themselves for a very long time. Against recently introduced plants such as strawberry guava and passionfruit vine, healthy rain forest might be able to hold its own. In contested terrain, on pig-disturbed ground, native species often cannot maintain their hold. Stricken, rain forest retreats before the invasion. And leading the invasion is the pig. Nothing stops the pig. To the Hawaiian rain forest, the pig is death.

It is death to the Hawaiian bog too. Every so often in rain forest you come unexpectedly upon a stretch of open country, the ground wet, the cover a low mat of hummocky sedges and grasses and curiously dwarfed trees and shrubs. Here heavy rainfall leaves the ground perpetually saturated. The bogs are islands of specialized growth within the rain forest. But to the feral pig a Hawaiian bog is just one more place to eat, offering something of a change of diet, earthworms and grubs again, but also scores of native lobelias and greenswords, showcase plants among the Hawaiian flora, some kinds of which are found in all the world only in these strange, secluded places. The pig snouts at the wet earth, churns the soil into muck with its hooves, and turns bog into piggery.

Everywhere the pig goes it loosens the spongy layers of moss that form the forest floor, producing slick mud, leaving wallows and little puddles of dirty standing water in which introduced mosquitoes can breed. This opens the way for yet another sickness to invade the rain forest, avian malaria, a killer of native birds.

And everywhere the pig goes, destroying the cover of the forest floor, it reduces the capacity of the rain forest to hold onto rain as it falls. One of the great, essential functions of these upland plant communities is to hold water in trust, so to speak, for the rest of the island terrain, capturing mist and fog,

ʻŌHIʻA LEHUA is the mainstay of Hawaiian forests; the dominant tree, its nectar is the source of life for a myriad of birds and other creatures.

buffering torrential rainfall, absorbing water and releasing it gently to aquifers and streams, reducing immediate flow in wet seasons, maintaining it in dry.

The primal vision of the rain forest is of a great, green regulative sponge, a vegetative heart pumping clear water year round forever, the water of life.

If intricately related communities of plants are disrupted and replaced by stands of a single plant like strawberry guava or passionfruit vine, watershed is put seriously at risk. If this single plant should be wiped out, say by disease, then the earth would be bare, stripped of its cover. Then water would seek its own level unimpeded, uncontrolled. Erosion could spread and destroy the land. So the pig rampant in rain forest and bog creates disaster not only in its immediate surroundings but everywhere downstream as well.

Water flooding unchecked out of ravaged rain forest scours loosened soil and dumps it in the ocean, suffocating coral reefs which used to be rich habitat for fish. On its way it crosses what has become increasingly the domain of other

feral animals that have gnawed and trampled their way
through native landscapes: cattle, goats, and exotic breeds
recently introduced as game for hunting—mouflon sheep,
blacktail deer, and Axis deer. From the mountains to the sea,
the words "feral ungulate" amount to a comprehensive curse
on the Hawaiian landscape, and the imprint of a cloven hoof
in disturbed and trampled soil is the mark of the beast.

DISRUPTION OF HABITAT means loss of species. In the forest
and bog country of Alaka'i on the island of Kaua'i there used to
be a big population of a native bird called the 'ō'ō. They were
described in 1891 as common, in 1903 as numerous, then by
1928 they were talked about as rare. By 1960 a survey could
find only twelve of them, and by the 1980s they were down to
two, and then to one—just like the Laysan teal, only this time
the circumstance is truly terminally dire, because the one
surviving Kaua'i 'ō'ō is a male, so that it is hard to envision
a miracle of biological brinkmanship in the Alaka'i. Wildlife
workers in the Alaka'i have spotted the last 'ō'ō in recent years,
each time in much the same place, one small black bird,
singing and building a nest each year, making all the right

moves of its species to attract a mate. But there seems to be no
mate to attract, and there probably can never be. The 'ō'ō was
photographed not long ago, in silhouette, alone. Its solitary
song was tape-recorded from up close and played back in the
forest the next day. The 'ō'ō, this lone black bird, flew to the
source of the song and found nothing but a single, wingless
black machine, singing.

*A ROBUST COIL of potential
growth will result in a frond over
ten feet long. The hāpu'u tree
fern of the Hawaiian rain forest
often creates a dense canopy
under a higher roof of native
trees, but they are slow growing,
taking over fifty years to reach
their full height.*

THE RICHNESS OF THE HAWAIIAN RAIN FOREST is captured in a small outburst of diversity under a single ʻōhiʻa tree growing in the Waiʻanae Mountains of Oʻahu. From the variety of mosses draping the branches to the tight cluster of native shrubs and ferns assembled beneath, we begin to feel the burgeoning presence of living things.

108

A FULL CANOPY OF FOREST spreads across the wet summit of Moloka'i, intercepting the rainfall, pulling moisture from passing clouds, bringing water to a thirsty island.

Following page: AS WILD AS ANY LANDS ON EARTH, remote Kipahulu Valley on Maui is clothed with rain forest; a refuge for endangered Hawaiian birds and a storehouse of biological riches.

SIPPING NECTAR FROM THE LEHUA BLOSSOMS, an 'apapane, the most abundant of the native Hawaiian honeycreepers, matches the color of the flower on which it feeds. Found on several of the main islands, 'apapane on different islands have developed dialects in their songs— the effect of island isolation on their continuing evolution.

THE FLASH OF RICH COLOR draws the eye to the Kamehameha butterfly, or pulelehua, one of only two native butterfly species in Hawai'i. It flits about conspicuously in wet gulches, pausing only to perch and spread its wings in the sunlight, basking for warmth in the cool mountain air.

OFTEN UNNOTICED ON THE MARGINS OF BOGS, the only carnivorous plant of Hawai'i is mikinalo ("fly-sucker"), a sundew also found in bogs worldwide. Glistening droplets on the ends of long hairs of its specialized leaves are sweet-smelling, but also a powerful glue that traps small flies and insects.

114

ONLY ALONG STREAMBEDS *are*
the ancient volcanic origins
revealed, but the basalt lava has
been sculpted into smooth, wet
forms, and the streambed is
framed with a soft green. This
is the climax—Hawaiian
rain forest.

BRILLIANTLY HUED, ACROBATIC AND BOISTEROUS, the 'i'iwi seems the ideal image of a Hawaiian honeycreeper. Its salmon-colored bill is curved to match some of the long-tubed flowers, such as the mā'ohi'ohi, from which it sips nectar. Still among the more common of Hawaiian forest birds, scientists watch it carefully. If the 'i'iwi begins to decline, how will rarer species fare?

WHEN KOLI'I BLOOMS, it is a wagon-wheel of magenta blossoms on a tall stalk. One of the celebrated Hawaiian lobeliads, famous as an example of island evolution, the flowers are visited by honeycreepers for their nectar, and they in turn depend on the birds for pollination. Ecological connections like these are everywhere in the Hawaiian rain forest, a vibrant, extensive network humming with life.

A BRIGHT FLAG ANNOUNCES NEW GROWTH for an 'ama'u fern. The red pigments, only seen in the young fronds, turn to a deep green as they mature. 'Ama'u ferns dominate some of the steeper slopes, too sheer for trees, and help protect the rain-drenched mountainsides against erosion.

118

Right: A MYRIAD OF FERNS drapes a wall, each has a name—hāpu'u, 'ama'u, and uluhe among them. In the rain forest, vegetation arranges itself in layers: ground-hugging mosses, through a tangle of shrubs and ferns, to a full crown of trees. It is a portrait that fills the senses.

A SILHOUETTE seen only in the Hawaiian rain forest, 'ōhi'a trees stand in the mist of a late afternoon.

PERHAPS THE MOST DISTINCTIVE of the Hawaiian honeycreepers, the 'ākohekohe is the only one that bears a crest of feathers on its head. Also known as the crested honeycreeper, it is one of the largest of the nectar-feeding Hawaiian birds, and can defend its favorite nectar trees from all other species.

122

WITH AN APT PROFILE, the rare Maui parrotbill is sometimes heard before it is seen, snapping twigs open with its powerful beak in search of tender grubs. It is known only from the high rain forests of northeast Haleakalā.

CLOUDS ROLL THROUGH A BANK of palaʻā ferns in an ʻōhiʻa forest near Kalalau Valley on Kauaʻi.

THE RAIN FOREST seems ready to spill over the steep windward cliffs of Moloka'i into the sea. Where undisturbed, the forest creates a continuous blanket of life, filling every available niche.

A HAWAIIAN RED HIBISCUS exhibits a frail beauty in the mild, nurturing climate of the wet forest.

A NATIVE WHITE HIBISCUS greets hikers on the quiet trails just above Honolulu, where wet forest of koa and 'ōhi'a can still be seen.

A FRIENDLY FACE awaits under the leaves of the rain forest. The happy-face spider is one of many uniquely Hawaiian animals living quietly and unnoticed, yet an integral part of the greater forest community.

A LILLIPUTIAN TERROR IN A FOREST PARADISE, an inch-long Hawaiian caterpillar munches on a startling meal—a native forest fly. The only predatory caterpillars known in the world, they were discovered through a lucky accident. A collector short on jars in the field added flies to a vial containing an innocuous-looking inchworm. When he next looked, this is what he saw.

126

BANDS OF FOREST colors ornament unhurried residents of Hawaiian forests. Tree snails carefully scour the leaves of their host trees, cleaning them of harmful algae and molds. In return they receive shelter from the elements, and a refuge from predators in the dense foliage.

THE PUREST WATERS have their beginnings high in the Hawaiian rain forest. With a priceless value as a living purifier, the watershed provided by rain forests such as Kamakou on Moloka'i may be the most important legacy for the future generations of Hawai'i.

128

A SUCCULENT PRIZE without the drawback of thorns, the 'ākala is a Hawaiian raspberry with large, delicious fruit. Because pre-human Hawai'i lacked large land mammals, many native plants have lost defenses such as thorns and poisons.

A LAST REFUGE, BUT NOT A LOST WORLD, the steep sides of Mount 'Eke have protected its pristine summit. Weed-free, pig-free, and rarely visited, it stands as an island of life in a sea of change. Even as pigs spread through the lowlands around it, fences are being built to keep the invaders from gaining the summit.

A GLORY OF THE MOUNTAINS is what the botanist thought, when he first saw the Lobelia gloria-montis. With a tall spire of white-petaled flowers, it graces the bogs and rain forests of Kaua'i.

LIKE AN ASSEMBLY OF EXTRATERRESTRIALS, a cluster of greenswords, closely related to silverswords, flowers simultaneously in a bog. Until recently this group of rare plants was in jeopardy from the depredation of pigs. Now, a sturdy fence protects them.

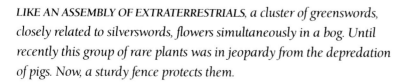

MORE LIKE ITS DESERT RELATIVE than its habitat would suggest, the West Maui silversword finds its adaptations to drought perfectly suited for the challenging conditions of the bogs atop the plateau of Mount ʻEke. Its closest kin, the Haleakalā silversword, has an identical growth-form.

TO THE HAWAIIAN RAIN FOREST, the pig is death: consuming ground-cover plants, churning the rich ground into foul muck, the forest dies from the bottom upward and the rains wash the soil away to smother coral reefs with silt.

A FERAL ANIMAL OUT OF PLACE IN HAWAI'I, the pig was a human introduction that has escaped into the wild. Unchecked by predators and spreading into areas that human hunters cannot reach, the pigs bring disease and destruction to Hawaiian forests.

A PROTECTED FOREST FLOURISHES in the Mount Ka'ala Natural Area Reserve on O'ahu. Fog-shrouded 'ōhi'a frames a pristine wilderness that persists even on the most densely populated of the Hawaiian Islands.

134

*WHEN WE ARE SENSITIVE
to the needs of ecosystems, our
structures complement the
natural contours of the land.
A wooden boardwalk in the
Kamakou preserve on Molokaʻi
protects the delicate bog community, while allowing us to
enjoy the beauty of the area.*

*A STRANGE, MINIATURE LANDSCAPE of low-growing sedges and
stunted trees, the bog at Pēpēʻōpae on Molokaʻi appears almost
magically in the midst of dripping rain forest. Dwarf ʻōhiʻa lehua
bloom within a mosaic of plants that is entirely native: a pristine
example of the Hawaiian montane bog.*

CHAPTER SIX
Summits

THERE IS A COLONY of dark-rumped petrels that spends part of the year on the summit of Haleakalā. Before dawn they launch themselves from their mountain home and glide thousands of feet down the wind to feed in the ocean. By night they make the arduous return flight: winging upward in the darkness, climbing through zone after zone of Hawaiian habitat—coast, strand, dryland, rain forest, the headwaters of streams. They bank over scattered *māmane*, the last of the upland trees. Higher still, trees give out altogether, unable to tolerate dry winds and icy temperatures, and the petrels traverse terrain densely packed with low, compact, tough, slow-maturing shrubs growing amid hardy grasses and sedges. Finally, at eight to ten thousand feet, the petrels of Haleakalā touch down in their home territory.

This is unmistakeably volcano country once more—rock, cinder, lichen. Here you are also above normal cloud cover, above the inversion layer, and the summits of Haleakalā on Maui and Mauna Loa and Mauna Kea on the Big Island appear to float on cloud banks—islands above islands.

Life at this altitude is hard. The extreme summits of Hawai'i are alpine stone deserts. The air is thin, the wind can blow blizzard-cold, and in some months of the year snow falls. At the highest of high altitudes, where even the soaring petrel rarely goes, life is ground down to mere flecks of biological being, tiny bugs with anti-freeze blood, some of them shaped to mimic their meager food supply, so that they can blow along with leaf litter and other plant debris into rock cracks to feed, safe out of the wind.

Life at the summit is not easy for human beings, either. The volcanologist Thomas Jaggar spent time at the extreme heights of the biggest volcanoes of the Big Island. But even he, Jaggar, an individual of world stature in a biological species of world stature, had to subsist at the top of Mauna Loa much like a *wēkiu* bug, in a rock crack roofed with iron sheeting. These days scientists are permanently and comfortably ensconced at high altitudes on the highest mountain of all, Mauna Kea. They are astronomers. They come from all over the world to this mid-Pacific summit because high-altitude Hawai'i is a place of remarkably clear air, the best for seeing into deep space, none better on earth.

Mauna Kea has huge telescopes funded at great expense by international scientific consortia, to look up and out, away from earth, to the planets and the stars. The astronomers do excellent work. Their scientific results are highly valuable to all humankind. No one would ever suggest otherwise.

It is just that in our time, late in the twentieth century— as conservation biologists are beginning to remark, with a certain irony—we have somehow come to know more about land surfaces light-years away in space than we know about the interior of rain forests on earth, including the rain forests of the island of Hawai'i, only a few thousand feet down the slopes of Mauna Kea from the giant telescopes.

HAWAIIAN SUMMITS ARE TROPICAL AND ALPINE at the same time. The juxtaposed habitats underscore the contrasts of Hawaiian ecosystems: high montane forests of koa and 'ōhi'a stand on the foothills of Mauna Kea, the tallest peak in Hawai'i. At 13,868 feet, its cinder cones are snow-covered in winter, and alpine conditions prevail year-round. Yet, less than five miles away, the Hawaiian tropical rain forest is burgeoning with a diversity of life.

ALWAYS THINK IN MILLIONS OF YEARS, urged Thomas Jaggar, and everything is in motion to one who senses slow motion.

This might be all very well for geologists, or for the astronomers of Mauna Kea, who think professionally in light-years. But those who think biologically about the Hawaiian Islands these days do not have such luxuries of time, and they might well wish that the rate of motion were far slower.

138 Consider the silversword. One of the splendors of the summit of Haleakalā is this plant of such strong and distinctive form, its rosette of silvery leaves glinting in the sun. It has always been the signature plant, the emblem, of Haleakalā. Visitors liked to take home a leaf, or more than one, or more than several—something special from a unique Hawaiian place, like a scorched Halemaʻumaʻu post card. And for the introduced goats on Maui, multiplying to tens of thousands on Haleakalā, silversword was truly excellent eating.

So picked at and picked over was the silversword that its future became doubtful. What began its rescue was the declaration of Haleakalā as a national park in 1913. Human beings were persuaded to be sparing of silversword leaves, and later on the goats were hunted and fenced out—down from tens of thousands to mere dozens.

But another enemy has crept into the park, unimpeded by fences and contemptuous of park rules and regulations. Undetected at first, the Argentine ant took up residence under rocks tenanted by ground-nesting, solitary native bees. Immediately, the introduced ants began eating the vulnerable larvae, and even the adult bees. For the silversword this was disastrous, because the bees are its essential pollinators.

These days it is possible to see silverswords in Haleakalā blooming by the hundred, a wonderful sight. But because of

THE FLOWERS of silverswords are a rare and spectacular explosion of color in a barren landscape of lava and cinder. Seven to twenty-five years of stored energy are spent in a single huge mass of flowers, each a fragrant daisy-like bloom.

the appetite of the Argentine ant, it is not possible to know whether abundant pollination is going to take place, whether enough seeds will be set to keep the population up at healthy levels. Native silversword remains hostage to introduced ant.

The only way to secure the survival of the Haleakalā silversword is for human beings to develop—and soon—management and control programs with more power than the singleminded and intimidating program of the Argentine ant.

All these episodes in the life of the silversword—flourishing untroubled, then stripped by humans and devoured by goats, then recovering within the benign confines of a park, then threatened by the invasion of the Argentine ant, with the realization of a continued future in peril—all this has happened in the space of only eight decades, a mere eye-blink in the biological life of the islands.

THERE IS AN ENIGMATIC saying that can be interpreted as a blessing or a curse: may you live in interesting times.

Certainly Hawaiʻi these days is an interesting place going through interesting times. Plant and animal species in great numbers have disappeared. But at the same time, species that have seemingly disappeared have been sighted again, sometimes after decades of presumed extinction. Perhaps even more surprisingly, in recent years a number of new species have been discovered, even on the densely populated main islands. And as recently as the last decade certain inconspicuous habitats have been recognized for what they are, home to whole communities of previously unobserved life forms: all the way from the anchialine pools, brackish enclosed ponds by the coast full of seaweeds and tiny shrimp that can turn the water red, to those strange lava tubes where little worlds of insects flourish in complete darkness.

Often—as with the *poʻouli*, a bird first sighted in rain forest on East Maui in 1973—the discovery that a species exists is simultaneously a discovery that the species is endangered. Interesting place, interesting times.

THE EARLY CHAPTERS OF THE STORY OF LIFE in the Hawaiian Islands concerned an intricate set of life forms evolving in splendid isolation. The chapter we are living out today concerns the breakdown of that isolation, and what happens to life forms confronted with momentous challenges from powerful outside forces.

What is happening in Hawaiʻi is happening all over the world. Everywhere on earth humankind is creating new "islands" of all sorts, from the Amazon basin to the rain forests of Southeast Asia to Yellowstone National Park. Everywhere man, for his own purposes, has been surrounding natural environments, isolating them and diminishing them. Everywhere the natural order of things has been rearranged to suit human purposes—cut up, divided, fenced, cropped, and cleared.

This makes for interesting times, and interesting times raise interesting questions. How do natural communities of plants and animals function when their surroundings are radically changed? How can native species be used to reclaim damaged landscapes and restore watersheds? How, for that matter, does rain forest flourish in poorly-drained soils that have apparently toxic levels of iron, manganese, and aluminum? South American forests yield a plant poison, curare, which has been "civilized" to become an invaluable medical anesthetic. A plant from Madagascar, the rosy periwinkle, yields an anti-cancer agent that can bring years of extra life to many children with leukemia. How much more of vital use to humankind remains to be discovered? On the

IN DELICATE CONTRAST to the harsh alpine setting, a Hawaiian geranium, nohoanu, grows in the summit shrublands.

139

highest level, what is the global effect of human intervention on such a sweeping scale in natural environments? Fundamentally, how can humankind strike the right balance between exploitation and preservation in a world of limited resources?

These are questions that show up most urgently on islands, where in the nature of things limits on resources are readily apparent and outside pressures are felt immediately and strongly. And nowhere can such questions be more clearly addressed than in the Hawaiian Islands. The biological history of the archipelago has stamped this place on the world map as conveying the absolute essence of island life, in all its isolated splendor and its vulnerability to invasion.

Just as Thomas Jaggar envisioned Hawaiʻi as a world center of volcanology, just as the Mauna Kea astronomers see Hawaiʻi as a world center of their universal trade, so it is possible to see a future for Hawaiʻi as a creative world center of conservation biology, solving local problems in a way that can be of significant use elsewhere in the Pacific and in other world regions.

Interesting place, interesting times, and the most interesting moment of time is right now. To stand on a Hawaiian summit and look outward is to have a vision of the whole natural world in rapid-motion change. That vision carries with it an irresistible invitation, one that in the nature of things can never be repeated, to live a genuinely interesting life; to help save, reclaim, and perpetuate a flourishing island of life upon the greater island of life which is the planet Earth.

*GROWING IN THE SAME HABITAT as silverswords, the related kūpaoa
assumes an entirely different life-form. A many-branched shrub with
sweet-smelling leaves (kūpaoa means "permeating fragrance"), it
contrasts strongly with the low silver rosette of the silversword; yet the
two plants are so closely related that they frequently hybridize.*

*AT ELEVATIONS ABOVE THE CLOUDS (left), the Hawaiian summits
receive little rain, so the forests there are marked by dryness. On the
uncommon occasions when clouds rise high enough, vegetation
intercepts airborne moisture, and fog drip is the major source of water.
Koa trees growing on the upper slopes of Mauna Loa show the
gnarled, twisting forms shared by trees at subalpine altitudes
worldwide. Instead of rain forest mosses and liverworts, the summit
trees are festooned with lichens that require the dry air.*

ONCE CLOSE TO EXTINCTION, the Hawaiian goose or nēnē was saved by a program of captive breeding and release. This relative of the Canada goose has adapted to a terrestrial lifestyle, and frequents the subalpine shrublands of Haleakalā on Maui. The highest summits are only an incomplete refuge for the ground-nesting nēnē: introduced predators such as rats and mongooses prevent them from living in the lowlands.

DEMONSTRATING ITS VERSATILITY, the 'ōhi'a lehua grows from near sea level to treeline above 7,000 feet. Scattered 'ōhi'a trees on the edge of Ko'olau Gap on Maui mark the transition from high montane forest to the subalpine ecosystems. Other subalpine plants, such as the 'ama'u fern and pūkiawe shrubs (foreground) dominate the slopes above the forest to the upper limits of vegetation at about 10,000 feet.

A SILVERSWORD spends most of its long life as a squat rosette of silver leaves. Then, within the brief span of a few months, it may quintuple its height as it sends a tall spike upward.

Left: A YOUNG SILVERSWORD and native bunch grasses break the seemingly sterile monotony of alpine cinderlands at Haleakalā Crater on Maui. The highest peaks in Hawai'i are also usually geologically young landscapes, where the latest round of volcanic activity has pushed lava from the earth's mantle upward. High above the effects of all but the most severe storms, the landscape is largely uneroded. The well-drained cinders provide footing for only a few species of hardy native plants.

IN FULL BLOOM, a mature Haleakalā silversword puts out a majestic arrangement of hundreds of flowering heads, then dies. Each head is composed of many individual flowers, so that thousands of windborne seeds may be produced. The parent plant never blooms again. Only a few of the seeds will find the rare patch of favorable habitat in which to start the slow cycle of life anew.

*AN EXPANSE OF HAWAIIAN TUSSOCK GRASSLAND grows on beds of
cinder from Haleakalā's last summit eruptions. It is one of the few
tropical subalpine grasslands on earth. Between the tussocks of the
Deschampsia grass a variety of native shrubs and ferns grow.*

THE PALILA LIVES AT THE HIGHEST ALTITUDE *of all of the Hawaiian honeycreepers. Its hefty beak is used to open the tough pods of the māmane, a yellow-blossomed native tree forming a forest ecosystem only in the summit cinderlands of Maui and Hawai'i. Like its honeycreeper relatives, the palila also sips nectar from the māmane blossoms, and feeds on a variety of native insects associated with the tree.*

INSISTENT MOUTHS AGAPE, *nestlings of palila are fed insects that are plentiful around the flowers and seeds of māmane trees. As long as there are healthy māmane forests, the endangered palila can endure.*

Following page: MAUNA LOA (THE "LONG MOUNTAIN") *is aptly named. Stark trunks of 'ōhi'a trees killed by volcanic ashfall stand as reminders that the Hawaiian Islands are still growing. It has taken over 10,000 cubic miles of lava, but only half a million years for this Hawaiian volcano to rise 13,000 feet above sea level.*

THE HIGHEST LAKE IN THE U.S., Lake Waiau is nestled in the crater of a cinder cone at 13,020 feet elevation, near the summit of Mauna Kea. It may have originally formed nearly 10,000 years ago, when the last ice age ended and the glacier that once capped Mauna Kea melted away.

NAMED FOR THE HIGHEST PEAK in the state (Pu'u Wēkiu on the top of Mauna Kea) the wēkiu bug is a wingless predator whose closest relatives of the lower forests are innocuous seed-eaters. Adapted to a snow-bound, alpine habitat, it has anti-freeze blood, and dark coloration that helps absorb warming sun for heat. Feeding on insects blown by winds up from adjacent habitat into the alpine cinderlands, the wēkiu bug lives off of a huge cache of frozen food. Such is the ecological network that runs from sea coasts to the highest summit peaks.

Right: THE MORNING SUN RISES ON A FROZEN SCENE high on the summit of Haleakalā, making it hard to accept that this is a landscape as "Hawaiian" as coastal dunes or tropical rain forests. With biological potential only recently recognized, the summits of Hawai'i represent exceptional opportunities for research.

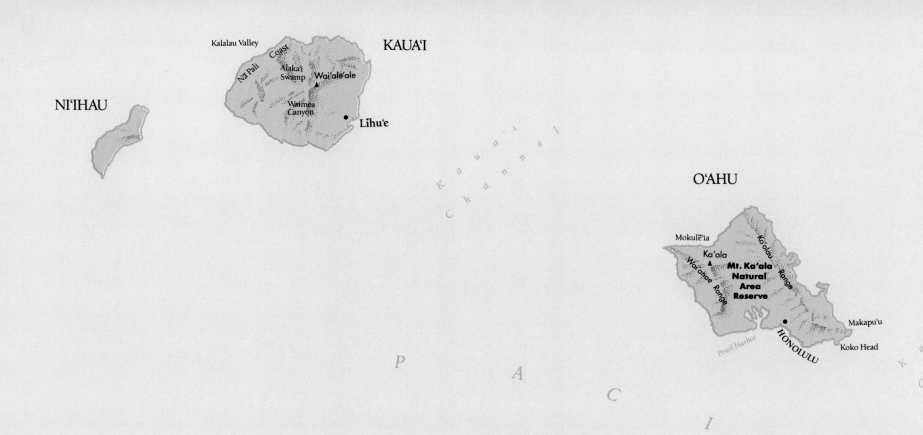

HAWAII: The Islands of Life

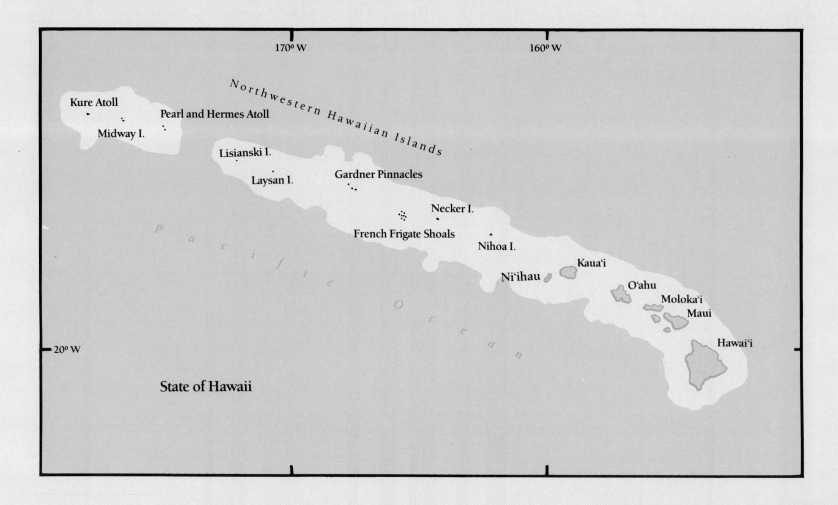

HAWAI'S ROLE IN THE EXTINCTION CRISIS

	HAWAII	PERCENTAGE OF U.S. TOTAL
LAND AREA	6,425 sq. miles	0.2%
NATIVE PLANTS & BIRDS	3,040	14.3%
ENDANGERED PLANTS & BIRDS	710	27.8%
EXTINCT PLANTS & BIRDS	251	72.1%

MOLOKA'I

Kalaupapa   Huelo Rock
Mo'omomi   **Pelekunu Valley**

Kamakou

Kaunakakai

MAUI

West   Eke Crater
Maui   **Wailuku**
Mtns.

Waikamoi
HALEAKALĀ   **Hāna**
NATIONAL
PARK
Haleakalā

'Ulupalakua

Kīpahulu

Kānepu'u

LĀNA'I   Lāna'i City

KAHO'OLAWE

Alenuihāhā   Channel

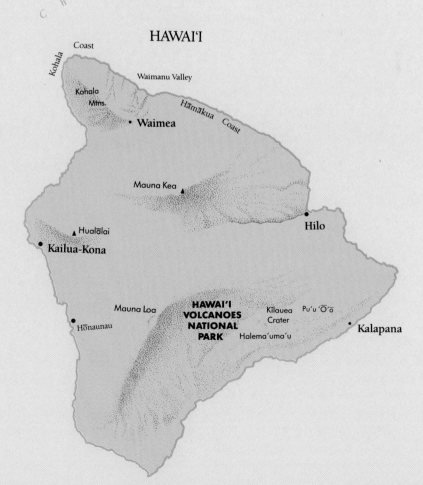

HAWAI'I

Kohala   Coast

Waimanu Valley

Kohala
Mtns.   Hāmākua   Coast

Waimea

Mauna Kea

Hualālai

Kailua-Kona   Hilo

Mauna Loa   **HAWAI'I**   Kīlauea   Pu'u 'Ō'ō
VOLCANOES   Crater
NATIONAL
Hōnaunau   **PARK**   Halema'uma'u   Kalapana

OCEAN

Photography Credits

154

Front cover ʻIʻiwi on ʻōhiʻa, rim of Kalalau Valley, Kauaʻi
David S. Boynton

Front flap New beach being created at Kupapau, Hawaiʻi Volcanoes
National Park—Peter French

Dedication

6 ʻAmakihi on koliʻi, forest above Kalalau Valley, Kauaʻi
David S. Boynton

8 Moʻomomi, Molokaʻi—Richard A. Cooke III

10 Waikolu Valley, Molokaʻi—Richard A. Cooke III

12 Hawaiian monk seal and Hawaiian green sea turtle,
Laysan Island—George H. Balazs

13 Sunrise, Molokaʻi—Richard A. Cooke III

14 The Hawaiian Islands seen from the Space Shuttle
Courtesy of NASA

Chapter One

16 Lava fountain, Hawaiʻi Volcanoes National Park
Richard A. Cooke III

19 Lava tongue, Hawaiʻi Volcanoes Nation Park
Dorian Weisel

20/21 Curtain of fire, Hawaiʻi Volcanoes National Park
Peter French

22 Curtain of fire, Hawaiʻi Volcanoes National Park
Greg Vaughn

23 Lava in forest, Hawaiʻi Volcanoes National Park
Dorian Weisel

24 Old lava at ocean, Kona, Hawaiʻi—Douglas Peebles
Lava into ocean, Kalapana, Hawaiʻi—Dorian Weisel

25 Nighttime lava into ocean, Kalapana, Hawaiʻi—Peter French

26/27 Puʻu ʻŌʻō vent, Hawaiʻi Volcanoes National Park
Lee Allen Thomas

28 ʻŌhiʻa lehua, Hawaiʻi Volcanoes National Park
John Eveland

29 Early fern growth, Hawaiʻi Volcanoes National Park
David Muench

30 ʻŌhiʻa forest, Saddle Road, Hawaiʻi—Jim Jacobi
ʻŌhelo berries, Hawaiʻi Volcanoes National Park
Greg Vaughn

31 Mature ʻōhiʻa forest, Hawaiʻi Volcanoes National Park
Greg Vaughn

32 Glowing lava tube, Hawaiʻi Volcanoes National Park
Dorian Weisel
Cave cricket, East Maui—William P. Mull

33 Lava tube, Hawaiʻi—Jim Jacobi
Surface cricket, Hawaiʻi Volcanoes National Park
William P. Mull

34/35 Lava landscape, Saddle Road, Hawaiʻi—Greg Vaughn

Chapter Two

36 Sea cave, Moʻomomi, Molokaʻi—David Muench

38 Morning glory, Moʻomomi, Molokaʻi—Richard A. Cooke III

39 Hinahina, Moʻomomi, Molokaʻi—Richard A. Cooke III

40 Laysan finch, Laysan Island—Stewart I. Fefer
Laysan teal, Laysan Island—Stewart I. Fefer

41 Laysan Island aerial—George H. Balazs

42 Frigate birds and Boobies, French Frigate Shoals
Bruce D. Eilerts

43 Albatross skycalling, Laysan Island—Frans Lanting

44/45 Puʻu Pehe cove, Lānaʻi—David Muench

46 Lithified dunes, Moʻomomi, Molokaʻi—David Muench

47 Beach plants, Wāwāmalu, Oʻahu—David Muench

48 Crab burrows, Moʻomomi, Molokaʻi—Ed Misaki
Turtle hatchling, French Frigate Shoals—Bruce D. Eilerts
Green sea turtles, French Frigate Shoals—Frans Lanting

49 Monk seal, French Frigate Shoals—Bruce D. Eilerts

50 Black noddy, French Frigate Shoals—Bruce D. Eilerts

51 Sooty terns, Pearl & Hermes Reef—R.J. Shallenberger

52 Red shrimp, Kona Coast, Hawaiʻi—Michael Lee

53 Luahinewai Pond, North Kona, Hawaiʻi—Greg Vaughn

54 Hāmākua coastline, Hawaiʻi—R.J. Shallenberger

55 Brighamia insignis blossom, Nā Pali Coast, Kauaʻi
Robert Gustafson
Brighamia on cliff face, North Coast, Molokaʻi
Steve Perlman

56 Coastal plants, Makapuʻu, Oʻahu—David Muench

57 Masked boobies, Kaʻula Rock, Kauaʻi—R.J. Shallenberger

58/59 Pelekunu Valley, Molokaʻi—Cindy Turner

60 Huelo Rock, Molokaʻi—Hugo DeVries

61 Nā Pali Coast, Kauaʻi—Frans Lanting

62 Marsilea villosa, Koko Head, Oʻahu—David Muench

63 Mokio Cliffs, Moʻomomi, Molokaʻi—Richard A. Cooke III

Chapter Three

64 Wiliwili, ʻUlupalakua, Maui—David Muench

66 Native hibiscus, Mokulēʻia, Oʻahu—John Obata

67 Wiliwili blossom, Waiʻanae Mountains, Oʻahu
John Eveland

68 Hawaiian hawk, North slope, Mauna Kea, Hawaiʻi
R.J. Shallenberger

69 Māmane tree, ʻUlupalakua, Maui—David Muench

70 Leeward Molokaʻi Mountains—Richard A. Cooke III

71 Wiliwili grove, Puʻu o Kalī, Maui—David Muench

72 ʻOhe ʻohe tree, Lānaʻi—David Muench

73 Gardenia seedlings, Kānepuʻu, Lānaʻi—David Muench

74 Lichen, South Slope, East Maui—David Muench

75 Euphorbia, Puʻu o Kalī, Maui—David Muench

76 ʻŌhiʻa lehua and lichen, Kapuʻa, South Kona, Hawaiʻi
Greg Vaughn

77 Pueo, Waimea, Hawaiʻi—Peter French
ʻAʻaliʻi, Hawaiʻi Volcanoes National Park—John Eveland

78/79 Evening light, Puʻu o Kalī, Maui—David Muench

80 Maʻo blossom, Hulopoʻe Bay, Lānaʻi—David Muench
Maʻo plant, Hulopoʻe Bay, Lānaʻi—David Muench

81	*Dry forest, 'Ulupalakua, Maui*—David Muench
82	*Sandalwood, 'Ulupalakua, Maui*—David Muench
83	*Wilkesia, Waimea Canyon, Kaua'i*—Greg Vaughn
	Wilkesia in bloom, Waimea Canyon, Kaua'i—Betsy Gagne
84	*Ash sand dune, Ka'ū Desert, Hawai'i*—Jim Jacobi
	Doryopteris, Auwahi, Maui—Robert Gustafson
	Hesperomannia, Wai'anae, O'ahu—John Obata
85	*Mixed dry forest, 'Ulupalakua, Maui*—David Muench

Chapter Four

86	*Pelekunu Stream, Kamakou, Moloka'i*—David Muench
88	*Plunge pool, Hāmākua Coast, Hawai'i*—Greg Vaughn
89	*Hawaiian stilt, Nu'upia Ponds, O'ahu*—R.J. Shallenberger
90	*Water seep, base of Mt. Wai'ale'ale, Kaua'i*—David Boynton
91	*Waimanu Valley, Hawai'i*—Greg Vaughn
92	*Stilts, Pearl Harbor National Wildlife Refuge, O'ahu* R.J. Shallenberger
93	*Dameselfly, Hanakāpī'ai, Kaua'i*—Jack Leishman
	Night heron, Hōnaunau, Hawai'i—Greg Vaughn
94	*Kohala Coast, Hawai'i*—Val Kim
95	*Kīpahulu, Maui*—Peter Menzel
96	*Gallinule, Wailua, Kaua'i*—R.J. Shallenberger
97	*Kapo'ikai Pond, Makalawena, Hawai'i*—Greg Vaughn
98	*Mt. Wai'ale'ale, Kaua'i*—Douglas Peebles
99	*Wai'ānapanapa Lake, Maui*—Gerald D. Carr
100/101	*Wailau and Pelekunu, North Coast, Moloka'i* Richard A. Cooke III
102	*Gobi, Kīpahulu, Maui*—Raymond A. Mendez
	Stream snail, Kīpahulu, Maui—Raymond A. Mendez
103	*Pelekunu Stream, Moloka'i*—David Muench

Chapter Five

104	*'Ōhi'a forest, Pu'u Ali'i, Moloka'i*—Jim Jacobi
106	*'Ōhi'a blossom, Hawai'i Volcanoes National Park* John Eveland
107	*Hāpu'u fern, Kamakou, Moloka'i*—Peter Menzel
108	*Rain forest, Wai'anae, O'ahu*—David Muench
109	*Kamakou aerial, Moloka'i*—Richard A. Cooke III
110/111	*Kīpahulu Valley, Moloka'i*—Peter Menzel
112	*'Apapane, Haleakalā, Maui*—Robert J. Western
113	*Kamehameha butterfly, Hawai'i Volcanoes National Park* William P. Mull
	Mikinalo, Alakai Swamp, Kaua'i—R.J. Shallenberger
114/115	*Kamakou Pool, Moloka'i*—Richard A. Cooke III
116	*'I'iwi, Waikamoi, Maui*—John Carothers
117	*Trematolobelia, Haleakalā, Maui*—Betsy Gagne
118	*'Ama'u fern, Kamakou, Moloka'i*—Ed Misaki
119	*Fern wall in rain forest, Moloka'i*—David Muench
120/121	*'Ōhi'a in sunset, Kōke'e, Kaua'i*—David Boynton
122	*Crested honeycreeper, East Maui*—Mark S. Collins
	Maui parrotbill, East Maui—Mark S. Collins

123	*Pala'ā fern, Kalalau Valley, Kaua'i*—David Muench
124	*Pelekunu trail, Moloka'i*—Richard A. Cooke III
125	*Red hibiscus, Wahiawa, Kaua'i*—Robert Gustafson
	White hibiscus, Tantalus, O'ahu—Robert Gustafson
	Happy-face spider, Hawai'i Volcanoes National Park William P. Mull
126	*Predatory caterpillar, Hawai'i Volcanoes National Park* William P. Mull
	Tree snails, O'ahu—Robert J. Western
127	*Kahanui Stream, Kamakou, Moloka'i*—Richard A. Cooke III
128	*'Akala, Kaua'i*—R.J. Shallenberger
129	*'Eke Crater, West Maui*—R. Alan Holt
130	*Lobelia gloria-montis, Kanaele Bog, Kaua'i* Robert Gustafson
	Greenswords, Upper Hana rain forest, Maui—Betsy Gagne
131	*'Eke silversword, West Maui*—Robert Hobdy
132	*Pig damage, Pu'u Kukui Maui*—David Muench
	Wild pig, Mauna Kea, Hawai'i—Tom Gillen
133	*Foggy forest, Ka'ala, O'ahu*—David Muench
134	*Kamakou Boardwalk, Moloka'i*—Win Anderson
135	*Pēpē'ōpae Bog, Kamakou, Moloka'i*—David Muench

Chapter Six

136	*Snow on Mauna Kea, Hawai'i*—David Muench
138	*Silversword blossom, Haleakalā, Maui*—Betsy Gagne
139	*Hawaiian geranium, Haleakalā, Maui*—R.J. Shallenberger
140	*Koa tree, Hawai'i Volcanoes National Park*—David Muench
141	*Kūpaoa, Haleakalā, Maui*—Betsy Gagne
142	*Nene geese, Pu'uanahulu, Hawai'i*—Greg Vaughn
143	*'Ōhi'a on pali edge, Waikamoi, Maui*—David Muench
144	*Native grass and silversword, Haleakalā, Maui* David Muench
145	*Young silversword, Haleakalā, Maui*—Betsy Gagne
	Silversword bloom, Haleakalā, Maui—Bill Tipper
146	*Alpine grassland, Haleakalā, Maui*—Robert J. Western
147	*Palila adult, Mauna Kea, Hawai'i*—Mark S. Collins
	Palila nest, Mauna Kea, Hawai'i—Charles Van Riper
148/149	*Mauna Loa Summit, Hawai'i*—Jeffrey Mermel
150	*Lake Waiau, Mauna Kea, Hawai'i*—Peter French
	Wēkiu bug, Mauna Kea, Hawai'i—William P. Mull
151	*Sunrise, Haleakalā, Maui*—Doug Peebles
Back cover	*'Ama'u fern/Hanakauhi, Waikamoi Preserve, Maui* David Muench
End sheets	*Dryopteris, Hāna, Maui*—David S. Boynton

Selected Readings

156

Attenborough, D. 1979. Life on Earth. Little, Brown and Company. 319 pp.

Berger, A. 1981. Hawaiian Birdlife. 2nd ed. Univ. of Hawaii Press, Honolulu. 270 pp.

Carlquist, S. 1974. Island Biology. Columbia Univ. Press, New York. 660 pp.

Carlquist, S. 1980. Hawaii: A Natural History. 2nd. ed. Pacific Tropical Botanical Gardens, Lawai. 468 pp.

Daws, G. 1974. Shoal of Time. Univ. of Hawaii Press, Honolulu. 494 pp.

Degener, O. 1975. Plants of Hawaii National Park. Reprint. Braun-Brumfield, Ann Arbor. 314 pp.

Sohmer, S. & R. Gustafson. 1987. Plants and Flowers of Hawai'i. Univ. of Hawaii Press, Honolulu. 160 pp.

Hawaii Audubon Society. 1986. Hawaii's Birds. 3rd ed., 2nd rev. Hawaii Audubon Society, Honolulu. 96 pp.

Kay, E. (ed.) 1972. A Natural History of the Hawaiian Islands. Selected Readings. Univ. of Hawaii Press, Honolulu. 653 pp.

Kepler, A. 1983. Hawaiian Heritage Plants. Oriental Pub. Co., Honolulu. 150 pp.

Kimura, B. & K. Nagata. 1980. Hawaii's Vanishing Flora. Oriental Pub. Co., Honolulu. 88 pp.

Lamoureux, C. 1978. Trailside Plants of Hawaii's National Parks. Hawaii Natural History Association. 80 pp.

Macdonald, G., A. Abbott & F. Peterson. 1983. Volcanoes in the Sea, The Geology of Hawaii. 2nd Ed. Univ. of Hawaii Press, Honolulu. 518 pp.

Merlin, M. 1976. Hawaiian Forest Plants. Oriental Pub. Co., Honolulu. 68 pp.

Pratt, H., P. Bruner & D. Berrett. 1986. Field Guide to Birds of Hawaii and the Tropical Pacific. Princeton Univ. Press, Princeton. 409 pp.

Rock, J.F. 1974. The Indigenous Trees of the Hawaiian Islands. Reprint of 1913 edition. Charles E. Tuttle, Rutland, VT. 548 pp.

Stone, C. & D. Stone (eds.). In press. Conservation Biology in Hawai'i. Univ. of Hawaii Press for CPSU/UH, Honolulu.

Stone, C. & J. Scott (eds.). 1985. Hawai'i's Terrestrial Ecosystems: Preservation and Management. CPSU/UH, Honolulu. 584 pp.

Tomich, P. 1985. Mammals in Hawaii. 2nd ed. Bishop Museum Press, Honolulu. 375 pp.

Van Riper, S. & C. Van Riper III. 1982. A Field Guide to the Mammals in Hawaii. Oriental Pub. Co., Honolulu. 69 pp.

Wagner, W., D. Herbst & S. Sohmer. In press. Manual of the Flowering Plants of Hawai'i. Univ. of Hawaii Press and Bishop Museum Press.

Hawaii The Islands of Life.

Produced by David Rick, Signature Publishing, Honolulu

Art Direction by Leo Gonzalez, The Art Directors Int'l., Inc.

Designed by Veronica Lam

Design Assistants: Jason Takaki, Kelly Fitzgerald, Juanita Buckley, Tadao Tanaka and Patrick Kalani Pa

Typesetting by Kellyjean Evans, Get Set Ltd.

Headline Type: Berkley Medium Italic

Subheads, Text and Captions: Berkley Book, Berkley Medium Italic and Berkley Bold Italic

Printed and bound in Tokyo, Japan by Toppan Printing Co., Ltd.